MAXnotes™

Zora Neale Hurston's

Their Eyes Were Watching God

Text by
Christopher A. Hubert
(B.A., Bates College)
Department of English
Oryol Pedagogical University, Russia

Illustrations by
Richard Fortunato

Research & Education Association

MAXnotes™ for
THEIR EYES WERE WATCHING GOD

Printed in the United States of America

Library of Congress Catalog Card Number 95-072124

International Standard Book Number 0-87891-053-0

MAXnotes™ is a trademark of
Research & Education Association, Piscataway, New Jersey 08854

I-1

What MAXnotes™ Will Do for You

This book is intended to help you absorb the essential contents and features of Zora Neale Hurston's *Their Eyes Were Watching God* and to help you gain a thorough understanding of the work. The book has been designed to do this more quickly and effectively than any other study guide.

For best results, this **MAXnotes** book should be used as a companion to the actual work, not instead of it. The interaction between the two will greatly benefit you.

To help you in your studies, this book presents the most up-to-date interpretations of every section of the actual work, followed by questions and fully explained answers that will enable you to analyze the material critically. The questions also will help you to test your understanding of the work and will prepare you for discussions and exams.

Meaningful illustrations are included to further enhance your understanding and enjoyment of the literary work. The illustrations are designed to place you into the mood and spirit of the work's settings.

The **MAXnotes** also include summaries, character lists, explanations of plot, and section-by-section analyses. A biography of the author and discussion of the work's historical context will help you put this literary piece into the proper perspective of what is taking place.

The use of this study guide will save you the hours of preparation time that would ordinarily be required to arrive at a complete grasp of this work of literature. You will be well prepared for classroom discussions, homework, and exams. The guidelines that are included for writing papers and reports on various topics will prepare you for any added work which may be assigned.

The **MAXnotes** will take your grades "to the max."

Dr. Max Fogiel
Program Director

Contents

Section One: *Introduction* 1

  The Life and Work of Zora Neale Hurston 1

  Historical Background 3

  Master List of Characters 3

  Summary of the Novel 5

  Estimated Reading Time 5

Each Chapter includes List of Characters, Summary, Analysis, Study Questions and Answers, and Suggested Essay Topics.

Section Two: *Their Eyes Were Watching God* 6

  Chapter 1 6

  Chapter 2 11

  Chapter 3 17

  Chapter 4 20

Chapter 5 26

Chapter 6 34

Chapter 7 41

Chapter 8 45

Chapter 9 50

Chapter 10 54

Chapter 11 57

Chapter 12 62

Chapter 13 65

Chapter 14 70

Chapter 15 75

Chapter 16 78

Chapter 17 82

Chapter 18 87

Chapter 19 93

Chapter 20 99

Section Three: *Sample Analytical Paper Topics* ... 104

Section Four: *Bibliography* 108

Introduction

The Life and Work of Zora Neale Hurston

Zora Neale Hurston was born in Eatonville, Florida. Her exact birthdate is unknown, but the most reliable sources put it at either 1891 or 1901. She was the daughter of John Hurston, a Baptist preacher, and Lucy Potts Hurston, a schoolteacher. Zora was the fifth of eight children, and in her autobiography, *Dust Tracks on a Road*, Hurston fondly remembers growing up in an eight-room house with "...two big chinaberry trees shading the front gate." Eatonville was a self-governing, independent, all-black town. Her father was mayor for three terms and helped codify the town laws. Hurston grew up believing that blacks were equal, if not superior to whites, and was very proud of her heritage. Hurston used her hometown as a basis for the fictional Eatonville in *Their Eyes Were Watching God* and even borrowed some real names for her characters.

Hurston came to New York in 1925 after receiving an Associate's Degree from Howard University. While at Howard, she was accepted into the prestigious campus literary group and published her first story, "John Redding Goes to Sea," in the campus magazine in 1921. In 1925, she submitted "Drenched in Light" to *Opportunity* magazine in New York, and it became her first nationally published piece. She then came to New York to continue her literary career. Hurston received a scholarship to Barnard and was its only black student; she graduated in 1928.

While at Barnard, Hurston developed an interest in anthropology. She studied for years and received several fellowships and grants. Her field of interest was folklore, and she used that extensively in her writings, always seeking to fuse folklore and fiction. *Their Eyes Were Watching God* was written in seven weeks while she was in Haiti working on a book about voodoo.

Hurston was one of the leading writers during the Harlem Renaissance, a period during the 1920s and 1930s when black writers came to the forefront of popular American culture. They were trying to repudiate the stereotypes of blacks in literature by bringing an individual character's consciousness to life. Through her associations with *Opportunity*, Hurston quickly became a popular guest at fashionable New York literary parties and became very friendly with Langston Hughes and other notable black writers.

Unlike many of her contemporaries, Hurston was nonpolitical and believed in art for art's sake. She wanted to express black folklore, which had long been rejected as a product of slavery, and bring it to a wider audience. In addition to her novels, Hurston wrote a play, an opera, several articles, and two anthologies of folklore. Her most famous article was called "How It Feels to be Colored Me," published in 1928.

Their Eyes Were Watching God, published in 1937, was Hurston's third novel. Sadly, the novel received mostly indifferent reviews when first released, including reviews by notable contemporaries. Many of her peers, such as Richard Wright, criticized the novel's lack of social relevance. They felt that the book was not pertinent in what Mary Helen Washington called "...a decade dominated by Wright and by the stormy fiction of social realism." Angered by the negative reviews, she began traveling again, and at the request of her publisher, wrote her autobiography in 1942. Her last novel, published in 1948 and called *Seraph on the Swanee*, was fueled by this anger and was about whites, not blacks. She felt she would be less open to criticism. Around the same time, Hurston was arrested and falsely accused of a morals violation. Although the charges were dismissed, she was demoralized and sick, and retreated to Florida. She spent the last years of her life in poverty, working in various odd jobs.

Zora Neale Hurston died on January 28, 1960. After her death, her books enjoyed a popular revival, partly due to the efforts of Alice Walker, who was greatly influenced by Hurston. Walker also edited and released a collection of Hurston's works. Today, Hurston remains one of the most influential black writers in America.

Historical Background

Hurston arrived in New York in the middle of the Harlem Renaissance. This was part of a historical process which altered black life in America, although it is usually thought of in literary terms. During the 1920s and 30s blacks were migrating to Harlem to escape the racism and oppression of the South. A community of blacks, was forming there and was attracting artists and intellectuals. When she first came to New York, Hurston became involved with *Opportunity*, a magazine dedicated to "New Negro thought," the thought that blacks would not accept a subordinate role in society. Hurston was very much a part of this group, and *Their Eyes Were Watching God* is, among other things, a story of a woman who refuses to be subordinate.

However, the only books by blacks that were critically well-received and big sellers during this time were books about the "race problem." Hurston didn't write about this. She tried to create a sense of black people as "complete, complex, undiminished human beings." For her lack of bitterness, she was seen as a traitor by some; others simply didn't take her seriously, calling her work "folklore fiction."

Additionally, many prominent blacks began to embrace communism, as it was the only political party that called for an end to segregation. Hurston stayed away from politics and was censured for it.

Their Eyes Were Watching God was severely criticized for being socially unimportant and actually detrimental to the black cause. Hurston's peers wanted to be part of the revolution; all she wanted was to tell her story.

Master List of Characters

Janie Crawford (Killicks, Starks, Woods)—*The protagonist of the story, a woman who searches for romantic love and equality in a male-dominated world.*

Tea Cake (Vergible) Woods—*Janie's third husband, a caring and fun-loving man who shares with Janie the romantic love she's been looking for.*

Joe (Jody) Starks—*The mayor of Eatonville and Janie's second husband. He treats Janie as property rather than his partner.*

Nanny—*Janie's grandmother. She brought Janie up after her daughter (Janie's mother) abandoned her. She forces Janie to marry Logan Killicks so that Janie will be protected.*

Johnny Taylor—*The young man who gives Janie her first kiss.*

Logan Killicks—*Janie's first husband, a farmer whom Janie was forced to marry and does not love.*

Pheoby Watson—*Janie's best friend. She is married to Sam Watson.*

Sam Watson, Lige Moss, and Walter Thomas—*Three men who endlessly talk in front of Joe Starks' store. Sam is Pheoby Watson's husband.*

Pearl Stone, Lulu Moss, and Mrs. Sumpkins—*Residents of Eatonville and gossip hounds who are envious of Janie.*

Lee Coker, Amos Hicks, and Tony Taylor—*Early residents of Eatonville.*

Hezekiah Potts—*The delivery boy of Joe Starks' general store.*

Hambo and Lum—*Two men who help around at Starks' store.*

Matt Bonner—*An Eatonville resident who sells a mule that he mistreated to Joe Starks.*

Mrs. Robbins—*A woman who always begs at Starks' store.*

Mrs. Bogle—*An old woman who lives in Eatonville.*

Rev. and Mrs. Pearson—*Eatonville's pastor and his wife.*

Charlie Jones—*A womanizer who lives in Eatonville.*

Daisy Blunt—*A pretty young woman who lives in Eatonville.*

Ike Green—*One of the many men who tries to marry Janie after Joe's death.*

Steve Mixon—*A customer who buys tobacco at Starks' store.*

Joe Lindsay and Jim Stone—*Customers at Starks' store*

The Washburn family—*A white family that lived in West Florida. Nanny was their servant and Janie lived with them when she was a young girl.*

Sop-de-Bottom, Ed Dockery, Bootyny, Stew Beef, Motor Boat—*Tea Cake's friends in the Everglades.*

Mrs. Turner—*Owner of a café in the Everglades. She is married and has a brother who is interested in Janie.*

Mr. Prescott—*A district attorney in the Everglades who prosecutes Janie for Tea Cake's death.*

Dr. Simmons—*A doctor who works in the Everglades. He tends to Tea Cake when he gets sick.*

Nunkie—*A woman in the Everglades who flirts with Tea Cake.*

Summary of the Novel

The novel begins with Janie returning to Eatonville after a long absence; she tells her story to Pheoby. Janie's story begins when she is a 16-year-old yearning to fall in love. Instead, her grandmother forces her to marry a local farmer, Logan Killicks, so that Janie will be protected from other men.

Janie is unhappy and runs off with Joe Starks, who she believes will give her what she wants. They move to Eatonville, where Joe becomes the first mayor and starts assuming complete control over Janie, never allowing her any fun or freedom. She becomes extremely disillusioned, and their marriage deteriorates.

After Joe dies, Janie meets Tea Cake, who is the first man to treat her as an equal. They fall in love and Janie leaves the comfort of Eatonville to go with Tea Cake to the Everglades. They have a lot of fun and are very happy together. Janie finally blossoms and enjoys the passion and splendor of life.

Unfortunately, Tea Cake gets bitten by a rabid dog while saving Janie's life during a storm. He soon goes mad and Janie kills him in self-defense. She is acquitted of murder by an all-white jury and goes home to Eatonville with the memory of Tea Cake.

Estimated Reading Time

The total reading time for the 184-page novel should be between six and eight hours. It is possible to read a few chapters at a single sitting, since most of them are less than ten pages long, and to finish the novel in three or four sessions.

Their Eyes Were Watching God

Chapter 1

New Characters:

Janie Crawford (Killicks, Starks, Woods): *the protagonist of* Their Eyes Were Watching God.

Pheoby Watson: *Janie's best friend who lives in Eatonville.*

Pearl Stone, Lulu Moss, and Mrs. Sumpkins: *Residents of Eatonville and gossip hounds who are envious of Janie.*

Summary

The sun is setting in Eatonville, Florida, and everyone is sitting around in front of their houses along the main road at the end of a long day. After a day at work, "it was the time to hear things and talk." Since the city is small, everyone notices the woman walking down the road.

The townspeople are shocked to see this woman coming through the city, apparently after a long absence. The men focus on how attractive she is while the women insult her clothing and say mean things about her. As she passes through the main road, she greets them pleasantly but quickly walks to her house and closes the gate.

As soon as she is out of earshot, the townspeople begin to speak about her and her return. It becomes clear that they resent her for some reason. We find out from a group of gossiping women that this woman, Janie, had left the town some time ago with a younger man. One of the women, however, begins to defend Janie against this gossip. Pheoby Watson was Janie's best friend while she was still in Eatonville, and she rushes over to Janie's house to welcome her back home and bring her some food.

Pheoby is warmly welcomed by Janie, and Pheoby immediately notices how well Janie looks now. Pheoby lets her know that the whole town is talking about her, and Pheoby also expresses her own curiosity about where Janie has been and what she has been doing. Janie lets Pheoby know that she is doing fine. She also tells Pheoby that she doesn't care at all about the rest of the town, or what they think. The only reason she is back in Eatonville is because Tea Cake, the man with whom Janie left, is "gone." Pheoby wants to hear more, because she is curious, but doesn't want to appear nosy. However, Janie wants to confide in her friend and is eager to tell Pheoby what has happened while she was away. So, Janie gives Pheoby permission to repeat the story if she wants, and tells her that she feels sorry for the other people of Eatonville, because while she was gone, she has been "a delegate to de big 'ssociation of life."

As the chapter ends, Janie is about to tell her story.

Analysis

As we notice from the first page, the language of the novel is very poetic. Hurston employs an omniscient narrator, which is a narrator that is able to see and hear things that a normal person could not, such as a character's thoughts. Instead of describing action, the narrator first explains the difference between men and women. According to the narrator, "ships at a distance have every man's wish on board." Some ships come to shore, and the man's wishes are fulfilled, while other ships stay away. Whether a man's wishes come true or not is a matter of luck, and the narrator says "that is the life of men." Women, on the other hand, "forget all of those things they don't want to remember, and remember everything they don't want to forget." In other words, women control their lives, because living in itself is the goal, and they don't waste time trying to chase down a dream that cannot be fulfilled. The narrator says that "the dream is the truth," and women "act and do things accordingly." Whether one agrees with the narrator or not, this difference will be what separates the female protagonist, Janie, from the men she encounters in the novel.

Another device that Hurston uses in her novel is colloquial speech. The characters speak in dialect, and Hurston writes the language as it is spoken. She does this in order to be more authentic and to make her characters real to us. The reader is then able to suspend his or her disbelief and to become emotionally involved in the characters' situations. Hurston wants the reader to feel for her characters because the story will have a stronger impact if the reader is sympathetic towards Janie, the heroine of the novel.

The relationship between Janie and the town of Eatonville is evident from the beginning of the novel. Even though we haven't learned Janie's name yet or the name of the town, Janie's situation immediately draws our sympathy. She is a woman, traveling alone, who is walking through a group of people who obviously don't like her. These people "sat in judgment," which is distasteful to us. Furthermore, Hurston utilizes metaphors in order to emphasize the cruelty of the townspeople. They "made burning statements with questions, and killing tools out of laughs." This language stresses the pain that words can sometimes cause, and anyone who has been insulted or bullied by words can understand the discomfort that Janie should feel in this situation. The fact that she is able to ignore this talk and greet them politely is courageous, and we admire her for this. The townspeople, on the other hand, only become more upset, and "hope that she might fall to her level some day." This statement is very ironic, because Janie's refusal to entertain the townspeople's nosy questions proves that she is, in fact, above them.

The three women who gossip as they see Janie coming down the street represent the jealousy that is rampant throughout the town. Pheoby Watson sees the hypocrisy in the town's moral code, and she understands that these women gossip about her friend because they are envious of her. Pheoby understands that the townspeople talk as if they "didn't do nothin' in de bed 'cept praise de Lawd." When Pearl Stone accuses Janie of "doin' wrong," Pheoby finally explodes, and points out that the real reason the town is mad at Janie is "'cause she didn't stop and tell us all her business." Her outrage at the town and her quick defense of her friend against these cowardly words makes the reader support her and Janie. Pheoby seems to be the only person brave enough to tell the truth in this town. Everyone else seems content to repeat the same evil-minded gossip.

When Janie greets Pheoby, she is very warm and genuinely glad to see her friend again. The two women talk very easily with one another, and their friendliness and kindness to each other is a direct contrast to the jealousy of the other residents. It is obvious to the reader that Pheoby was correct in defending Janie, and the thought that Janie did something wrong is completely unjustified. Janie is just as aware of the attitude of the town as Pheoby was and refers to the people collectively as "Mouth-Almighty." This image reinforces the idea that Janie and Pheoby are the only two people in the town who are worthwhile enough to express their own opinions. The other townspeople just speak without thinking.

So, the purpose of the first chapter is twofold: first, to introduce the character of Janie to make the reader interested in Janie's story, which will be told in the following chapters; second, to establish a conflict between Janie and the townspeople, which is an example of the sort of conflict Janie has had to fight all her life. She has spent her life fighting against what other people expect and want from her. The reader identifies with Janie rather easily because it is the same sort of conflict that most people experience. The reader finishes the first chapter looking forward to Janie's story.

Study Questions

1. According to the book, what has the woman come back from doing?

2. Why did all the people see her come?

3. What do they remember about the woman?

4. What do the men notice about Janie as she walks down the street, and what do the women notice about her?

5. What does Pheoby bring for Janie?

6. What is Janie doing as Pheoby walks in?

7. According to Sam Watson, why do the residents of Eatonville want to rise on Judgment Day?

8. Why does Sam want to rise as well?

9. Does Janie intend to tell the residents of Eatonville what happened while she was gone?

10. What does Janie mean when she says "unless you see de fur, a mink skin ain't no different from a coon hide?"

Answers

1. The woman has come back from "burying the dead."

2. Everyone could see the woman because the sun was going down, and everyone had finished work and was sitting outside.

3. They remember the envy they felt when she left.

4. The men notice her beautiful body and long hair, while the women notice her filthy clothes.

5. Pheoby brings a plate of mulatto rice for Janie.

6. Janie is soaking her feet in a pan of water.

7. Judgment Day is supposedly the day when all the secrets will be made known. Sam thinks that all of Eatonville goes to church just so that they can rise to Heaven and have something new to talk about.

8. Sam wants to find out who stole his corn-cob pipe.

9. Janie only intends to tell Pheoby because "tain't worth de trouble" to tell anyone else.

10. Janie starts to tell her story to Pheoby, but she tells it in such a disorderly fashion that Pheoby has a hard time understanding her. Janie decides that "tain't no use in me telling you somethin' unless Ah give you de understanding to go 'long wid it." The skin of a mink and a (rac)coon are the same without the fur. Janie meant that it is hard to know something if you don't know the complete picture.

Suggested Essay Topics

1. How does Pheoby's moral code differ from the moral code of the town? Which code is truly "moral"?

2. Do you agree with the first two paragraphs of this chapter? Explain why you agree or disagree with the narrator.

Chapter 2

New Characters:

Nanny: *Janie's grandmother. She brought Janie up after her daughter (Janie's mother) abandoned her. She forces Janie to marry Logan Killicks so that Janie will be protected.*

Johnny Taylor: *A young man who kissed Janie.*

The Washburn family: *A white family who lived in West Florida. Nanny was their servant and Janie lived with them when she was a young girl.*

Summary

Janie's recollections take her to her childhood, when she grew up with her grandmother, who was a live-in servant for a white family. One of her favorite memories is of sitting under a peach tree when she was a young woman, and it is under this tree that she first kisses a boy. Her grandmother sees her kissing Johnny Taylor and tells her to come inside. Janie leaves Johnny and comes into Nanny's bedroom, where Nanny is lying in her bed.

Janie's grandmother is very scared for her, because she is at a vulnerable age where any man can take advantage of her. Janie tries to calm down her grandmother, but Nanny says she has already arranged for Janie to marry Logan Killicks, a local farmer. Janie isn't ready for marriage and certainly does not want to marry him, but doesn't know how to tell her grandmother.

Nanny can understand why Janie is upset, so she tries to explain to Janie why she decided this must be done. Nanny takes Janie in her arms and tells her of her own life. When she worked in Savannah as a slave, she fell in love with her master's son, and they

had a child. However, after the son went to fight for the Confederacy, Nanny had to escape for fear of her child. Janie's mother, however, wasn't very stable, and abandoned her own daughter with Nanny so she could go out drinking. Nanny is scared that something like that will happen to Janie, so she begs her to marry Logan so that she might have something to own. She tells Janie that "she can't die easy thinkin' maybe de menfolks white or black is makin' a spit cup out of you."

Analysis

We can see that Janie has had trouble with her own identity from the very beginning of her life. She wasn't even aware of the fact she was black until she saw a picture of herself, and this revelation is thought to be funny by the other members of the family with whom she lives. This sort of identity crisis affects her childhood deeply. She wore clothes that the Washburn family gave her, which made her a target of ridicule for the other black girls. Janie has trouble finding out what sort of person she is because of this identity conflict. Her peers are envious of her nice clothes, which they identify as clothes of the rich, even though Janie is not rich herself. The other children ostracize Janie by telling her that her father was hunted by the police. As Janie tells this to Pheoby, she clearly is still upset over how the children treated her, and she complains that "dey made it sound real bad so as tuh crumple mah feathers." The children had used Janie's father to offset the pride she had felt by wearing nice clothes. They also showed Janie the power of society, which is an important theme that runs through the novel, and the way this power can be used to make an individual feel inferior.

Chapter 2 begins in the first-person; the story is told from Janie's point of view in her own words. She is the one who tells this story to the reader, rather than the omniscient narrator (Hurston). After this anecdote is told, the novel switches back to the third-person point of view. It was important that we hear this story in Janie's words, since her feelings are what gives the anecdote its impact. This story is an example of the battle for her self-esteem that Janie fights throughout her life, and its importance is emphasized by being narrated in her own words.

One of her first memories is a pear tree under which she always chose to rest. Janie, for some reason, feels an unusual attachment to the "blossoming" tree. One day, as she sits under the tree, she watches a bee pollinating a flower. After watching this, she understands why she has been spending so much time in the garden. "She had been summoned to behold a revelation." This act is a powerful image, since it symbolizes a "marriage" in Janie's eyes. This bee and flower are symbols, which are juxtaposed against man and woman. It is the duty of these natural beings to perform this beautiful act, and Janie starts to feel that this nature is also inside her. She feels about herself as "a pear tree in bloom...with kissing bees singing the beginning of the world!" After receiving this knowledge, she wants to imitate the flower, and finds Johnny Taylor coming up the garden path.

Janie's kiss is as innocent as the nature of the bee and the flower. To Janie it is simply a way to celebrate her new found nature. However, it terrifies Nanny, who sees them from her bedroom window. Janie's explanation doesn't help, because it is Janie's innocence that concerns Nanny. Nanny wants to make sure that Janie is married before some other man takes advantage of her, which is why she accepted Logan Killicks' proposal on her behalf. Janie does not want to go against Nanny, although "the vision of Logan Killicks was desecrating the pear tree." Janie cannot see herself married to this man; this marriage of convenience contradicts her ideal vision.

Nanny slaps Janie out of fear that she will refuse, and tries to calm her down by telling her the story of her own mother. Janie's mother was only 17 when she was raped by Janie's father, and Nanny is afraid that she will "see it all over again." Nanny's sufferings were horrible, and she doesn't have the strength to see what happened to her daughter happen to Janie. She tells Janie that she "don't want yo' feathers crumpled by folks throwin' up things in yo' face."

This story is told to establish Nanny's fear. Her experiences have convinced her that it is necessary for a woman to be safe. She sees Janie as an innocent who is susceptible to victimization as her own daughter was victimized. To Nanny, the marriage to Logan is a respectable solution. While Janie's new feelings are strong, she

gives in for her grandmother's sake, since her battles with society from childhood have left her without the confidence to follow her feelings.

Study Questions

1. Why is it hard for Janie to start her story?

2. Why was Janie called Alphabet?

3. Why had Janie been spending so much time underneath the pear tree?

4. Who is the "glorious being" that Janie sees coming up the road?

5. Why is Nanny scared for Janie?

6. Why does Nanny want Janie to marry Logan Killicks?

7. What happened to Nanny's lover?

8. Why did Nanny run away from the plantation in Savannah?

9. Who was Janie's father?

10. Why does Nanny call herself a "cracked plate"?

Answers

1. Janie finds it hard to begin since her early childhood has been so hard to remember.

2. Everyone had called her so many different names up to that point.

3. Ever since the pear tree began to bloom, "it had called her to come and gaze on a mystery." Janie is enamored with the tree and loves to sit under it and listen to the bees among the flowers.

4. The "glorious being" is Johnny Taylor, who was "shiftless" in Janie's "former blindness."

5. Janie is a woman now, and Nanny feels that Janie will be an easy target for any man who wants to take advantage of her.

6. Nanny wants Janie to marry for "protection."

7.   Nanny's lover went to fight in the Civil War. Nanny never saw him again.

8.   Nanny's mistress knew about the affair between Nanny and her husband. After the master leaves, the mistress beat Nanny and threatened her with a whipping and the loss of her child. Even though Nanny was weak from her recent childbirth, she was scared to stay on the plantation.

9.   Janie's father was a schoolteacher who had Janie's mother as a student. He raped Janie's mother when she was 17.

10. Nanny has had a very difficult life which left her vulnerable and frail. Now that she is old and doesn't have the strength to fight people, she asks Janie to have mercy on her and marry Logan.

Suggested Essay Topics

1.   Write a paragraph from Nanny's point of view, explaining and justifying her arrangement between Janie and Logan Killicks.

2.   The pear tree is one element of nature in this chapter. What other symbols of nature can you find?

Chapter 3

Summary

Janie is left to think about her marriage to Logan Killicks. She wonders about the connection between love and marriage, but convinces herself that they will love each other after they are married. They are married at the Washburn place, and Janie leaves to live at the Killicks' farm. After two-and-a-half months, Janie returns to Nanny for advice. She lets her know that she is not satisfied with the marriage. Logan isn't a cruel man, but Janie is bored, and he is too callous to see that she is unhappy with him. Nanny advises Janie to be patient and that it is "better [to] leave things de way dey is," since Janie is still young. So, Janie returns to Logan, prepared to wait for things to improve. A month later, Nanny dies. Janie continues to wait, but as time goes on, she only realizes that "marriage did not make love." Having realized this, she "became a woman."

Analysis

This short chapter shows the reader that Janie's doubts about marrying Logan Killicks were justified. She spends her time underneath the pear tree, wondering about the marriage. Her connection with nature is the reason she still feels doubt. Her idea of marriage is the bee mating with the flower. She reaches a logical conclusion which helps her soothe her fears; since marriage is natural, she should be happy when she is married. Once she is married, however, this is clearly not the case.

Janie is unable to find any consolation from Nanny. In her conversation with Nanny, the reader sees that her expectations were much different from Janie's. Nanny's first concern is that Logan has been abusing her, and when Janie tells her differently, Nanny wonders what could be upsetting her. Nanny has pushed Janie into a stereotypically female role. In Nanny's ideal of a marriage the woman is a housekeeper, while the husband is the provider. Therefore, she cannot understand the source of Janie's unhappiness, because Nanny connects marriage with safety, not love. Nanny thinks of love as "de very prong all us black women gits hung on." To Nanny, love is an abstract idea that causes the vulnerability that she is so afraid of. So she simply points out to Janie (once again) that Logan is the richest black man in the area, and therefore, a good source of security.

While Janie returns out of respect for her grandmother, Nanny's death has another profound effect upon her. Nanny gets her wish; her granddaughter doesn't need her protection anymore. However, since Janie was married to Logan in the first place to satisfy Nanny, there is no longer a reason to continue. Janie had followed Nanny because she lacked the self-esteem to follow her true feelings. Without Nanny, Janie no longer has a person to follow, since she cannot bring herself to follow Logan.

So Janie finds herself unsatisfied, and finds out that her earlier instinct was the correct one. She "became a woman" because her "first dream was dead." While she is disappointed now, she has now become wiser due to this disappointment. Nanny's death has at least given her the freedom to live without worrying about hurting someone she loves. She will explore this freedom in the next chapter.

The language of the novel as Janie waits to be happy is filled with symbols of nature, since the natural world offers Janie refuge from the society that imposes roles upon her. She claims to understand "the words of the trees and the wind," and finds acceptance in this world. This realm of nature will be another important image in this novel.

Study Questions

1. What does Janie ask herself as the marriage approaches?

2. Who arranges Janie's wedding ceremony?

3. When Janie asks Nanny for "information" why does Nanny laugh?

4. What does Janie want Nanny to do?

5. What does Nanny mean when she says "bein' a fool don't kill nobody. It just makes you sweat"?

6. What doesn't Janie like about Logan's appearance?

7. What does Nanny do after Janie leaves her?

8. What is "a bloom time, a green time, and an orange time?"

9. What does she tell the seeds, and why?

10. What "failed" Janie, and what does she do about this?

Answers

1. Janie wants to know if marriage will "compel love like the sun the day." She also hopes that marriage will end her loneliness.

2. Nanny and Mrs. Washburn take care of everything.

3. She guesses that Janie might already be pregnant.

4. She wants Nanny to tell her how to love Logan.

5. According to Nanny, love is what keeps a woman "pullin' and uh haulin' and uh sweatin' and doin' from can't see in de mornin' till can't see at night." She considers such behavior foolish, because to her love isn't realistic, and it is senseless to worry oneself over it.

6. According to Janie, he is too fat, "his toe-nails look lak mule foots," and he doesn't wash himself enough.

7. After Janie leaves her, Nanny goes to her shack and prays the entire night.

8. These "times" are the seasons that pass as Janie waits for her marriage to improve.

9. She tells the seeds, "Ah hope you fall on soft ground," because she had heard seeds say that to each other.

10. Janie looks up the road that passes her gate because "the familiar people and things had failed her." She looks for something new and exciting to come along and rescue her from this familiarity.

Suggested Essay Topics

1. Describe how Janie comes to the conclusion that "marriage did not make love."

2. Do you think that Nanny was satisfied with Janie's marriage at the time of her death? Use examples from the book to support your position.

Chapter 4

New Characters:

Logan Killicks: *Janie's first husband, a farmer whom Janie was forced to marry and does not love.*

Joe (Jody) Starks: *A savvy businessman from Georgia who meets Janie along the road.*

Summary

A few months have passed since Nanny's death, and Janie notices that Logan has been treating her with less respect. Logan begins to resent Janie's unhappiness, and feels that she thinks she is better than he is. He decides that she has been "spoiled" by her grandmother and that she expects him to continue spoiling her.

One day, Logan heads into town with the intention of buying a new mule, implying to Janie that she will have to help him in the garden next year with the new crops.

While Logan is in town, Janie, working in the garden, sees Joe Starks coming up the road. Janie begins to pump water in order to attract his attention, and Joe asks her for a drink. He is on his way to Florida because he has heard of a city that will be run by blacks, and he intends to be a big man in that city. Joe immediately charms Janie with his words and his style. Janie enjoys having someone to keep her company and they begin to see each other regularly. After a week, Joe proposes to Janie and offers to take her with him to this new town in Florida.

That night, Janie asks Logan what would happen if she decided to leave him. Logan had been afraid of this, but pretends that he doesn't care in order to hurt her feelings. The next day, Logan asks Janie to help him with work outside and accuses her of cheating on him when she refuses. Janie simply ignores him, however, and quietly leaves the farm and heads to the place where she knows Joe is waiting for her. As the chapter ends, Janie and Joe are already married and preparing to leave for Eatonville.

Analysis

Since the reader has already read about Logan in the previous two chapters, we already expect that he is an unpleasant man. As a result of this foreshadowing, our first impression of Logan is already conceived, and his first appearance in the novel doesn't challenge our expectations. Logan feels that Janie thinks herself to be better than him, but since we have already experienced this sort of feeling about her from the residents of Eatonville in Chapter 1, we immediately sympathize with Janie and identify him with her earlier enemies. Logan shows himself to be the same type of person that Janie and Pheoby disliked, by sharing the same restrictive view of Janie with "Mouth-Almighty."

Janie's first meeting with Joe Starks serves as a contrast to the life that Janie has been living and to the person with whom she has been living. From the conversations they have, Joe can easily see that Janie is unhappy and dissatisfied. By commenting on her youth and telling her about his own dreams, Joe easily influences her. Janie, in return, wants to be influenced, since it is a welcome change from the drudgery that she has experienced with her unsympathetic husband. Joe's ambitions give Janie an alternative, something she can now follow instead of Logan's orders.

She does not know if Joe is her ideal man, which is why she "pulled back" after Joe's talk of marriage. Joe "did not represent sun-up and pollen and blooming trees," which are symbols the reader has identified with Janie. What he does represent, however, is "change and chance," which is in itself enough for Janie right now. "Change and chance" are at the very least, abstract concepts which excite her. Logan's future is very concrete and secure, and also very boring for her. However, Janie's commitment to Logan is still strong despite her unhappiness. This is not because she loves him, but because her idea of marriage insists that she remain faithful. Furthermore, "the memory of Nanny was still powerful and strong" for her, and this obligation also makes Janie hesitant.

So, even though she is tempted to move away with Joe, she still gives Logan an opportunity to convince her to stay. Janie's conversation with Logan in bed is an important scene because Janie shows her true character. Even though she has had to endure their marriage from the very beginning, she still treats their marriage seriously enough to give him a chance to say or do something to show that a mistake hasn't been made. Logan, as the reader might have expected, reacts very defensively, because he has had the same fear himself. Instead of confronting this fear, however, he makes a rather half-hearted attack upon her family, in the same sort of way the gossip hounds of Chapter 1 refused to confront their true feelings. Logan shares the same sort of ideas about marriage with Nanny. His wife should be content to work for him while he maintains his position as head of the household. His anger stems from the belief that Janie should appreciate his possessions and the fact that he chose to marry her.

Janie isn't so easily contented, but Logan decides to impose his authority and order her around more strictly. The next day, Logan orders Janie to stop cooking to help him shovel manure, a degrading task for her that would prove that Logan is the head of the household. Janie, of course, refuses, and also lets Logan know how she really feels about their marriage. Logan isn't so honest with Janie in return, and replies with a bitter attack upon her and her family. During all this abuse, however, Janie doesn't become offended. She is now convinced that "even if Joe was not there waiting for her, the change was bound to do her some good." As she walks through the open air, she takes off her apron, which represents not only her obligation to work but also her obligation to both Logan and Nanny.

We can tell by the end of the chapter that Janie's concerns about marrying Joe are temporarily forgotten in this new found freedom. Joe is called "a bee for her bloom," which emphasizes that Joe is Janie's own choice and therefore a "natural" marriage. Because Janie wants to feel as if she is pursuing her own destiny, she juxtaposes her ideal of marriage upon Joe. Of course, there are still doubts as to whether Joe will be any better, but like Janie, the reader temporarily forgets about him because Janie has bravely ended her marriage to Logan. Janie was not satisfied with her current situation and ignored her grandmother's and Logan's stereotypes in hope of a better future. The reader enjoys Janie's victory, and also looks to the unknown future to provide the answers.

Study Questions

1. How does Logan treat Janie differently in the months that follow Nanny's death?

2. What does Janie do when Logan threatens not to chop any wood for her?

3. Why does Logan want an extra mule?

4. Describe Joe as Janie first sees him.

5. As Joe walked down the road, "he acted like Mr. Washburn or somebody like that to Janie." What does this imply?

6. Why does Joe want Janie to shake her head?

7. What does Janie mean when she says to Logan, "you don't take nothin' to count but sow-belly and cornbread"?

8. Why does Logan ask Janie to come to the barn while she is in the middle of cooking breakfast?

9. What does Logan look like with a shovel in his hand?

10. According to Janie, why is Logan mad at her words?

Answers

1. Logan has stopped talking in rhyme to her, and he no longer plays with her hair.

2. Janie tells Logan that if he stops chopping wood, she won't make him any dinner.

3. He wants to have a large potato crop, and expects Janie to help him plow with one of the mules.

4. Joe was "seal-brown," "cityfied," and "stylish dressed." He had on a silk shirt, with his coat hanging from his arm. His hat was worn at an angle, which indicated that he "didn't belong in these parts."

5. Joe's confident stride is something that Janie has seen only in Mr. Washburn, and in her mind, that confidence is only in people who possess some sort of power. She is immediately interested in Joe because she has never seen a black man act with such confidence.

6. Joe loves to see Janie's long hair move back and forth when she shakes her head.

7. Logan is concerned more with his crops and his farm than with his wife. As long as his dinner is made every night, it seems to Janie that anyone could be his wife.

8. Logan wants Janie to help him move a pile of manure into the barn.

9. Logan looks like "a black bear doing a clumsy dance on his hind legs" with a shovel in his hand.

10. Janie says that Logan is mad at her because he already knows that she doesn't consider him or his land important. She also doesn't feel the gratitude that he apparently expected from her. As she tells him how she feels, she also tells him that he shouldn't be so mad because he already knew all of this.

Suggested Essay Topics

1. Write about an important decision that you made in your life and describe how you felt when you made that decision.

2. Could Logan have kept Janie from leaving him if he had truly told her how he felt? Use examples from the chapter to support your decision.

Chapter 5

New Characters:

Lee Coker, Amos Hicks, and Tony Taylor: *Early residents of Eatonville.*

Sam Watson: *A man who endlessly talks in front of Joe Starks' store. Sam is Pheoby Watson's husband.*

Sim Jones, Jeff Bruce, and Oscar Scott: *Three residents of Eatonville.*

Mrs. Bogle: *An old woman who lives in Eatonville.*

Summary

As the chapter begins, Janie and Joe are on the train to the new town. Janie is impressed with Joe's demeanor and attitude, which she thinks is "like rich white folks." Joe buys her presents, but is more excited about arriving and starting to work on the ideas he has spent so long preparing. However, once they arrive in Eatonville, they discover that it is nothing more than a few houses and 50 acres of land. Neither one of them can hide their disappointment about the town, but Joe nevertheless begins to think about how he can start his plans.

Joe tries to find the mayor, only to find out from a couple of residents that the town doesn't have one. Joe then takes it upon himself to call a meeting of the residents. At this meeting, he announces his attention to buy extra land and build a store in the center of town. This causes the townspeople to laugh out loud, but they soon stop laughing when Joe buys 200 acres of land in cash.

After this surprise, they begin to organize themselves with Joe as the unspoken leader. Everything happens so quickly it is hard

for Janie to keep up with Joe. Before she knows it, the store is also finished. At the party celebrating the store's opening, Joe Starks is elected mayor of Eatonville in an outburst of support from the townspeople. Joe gets up and gives a little speech with pride. When Janie is asked for a few words, however, Joe quickly interrupts, saying that Janie is "uh woman and her place is in de home." Janie feels a little scared after this unexpected outburst but says nothing.

The town grows with Joe as its leader, and another party is held when the first street lamp is installed in the Eatonville streets. The arrival of light on the city streets at night is welcomed by its residents, and Joe walks home with more pride than ever. Janie, however, tells her husband how lonely she feels and how she hopes "it soon gits over." Joe can't believe what he hears from Janie and replies that he "ain't even started good." While he tells her about his dreams once again, Janie becomes truly afraid.

In a very short time, however, Joe Starks is the most powerful man in Eatonville. Janie learns that "the wife of the Mayor is not just another woman as she had supposed." Meanwhile, the other residents of Eatonville have looked at Joe in a new light. The town looks at him not only with respect, but also with fear and hatred. The chapter ends with a group of men talking about Joe and the sort of man he is. The debate is heated, with some people hating the control that Joe seems to have over the town. As an afterthought, the men discuss Janie and how Joe treats her so harshly whenever she makes a mistake. This conversation, however, is soon settled when one man guesses that "dey understand one 'nother."

Analysis

The chapter begins with a lot of hope, especially on Janie's part. The reader has just witnessed Janie take a great risk in her life, and we naturally hope that it pays off. Joe seems a little excited as well, although his talk is centered on the town rather than their marriage. Janie is more than content, however, probably because the excitement is a welcome change from the boredom in her marriage with Logan. Even though they are not specifically her dreams and desires, she is happy for the time being, to share Joe's excitement and dreams.

When they first arrive, they share their disappointment. As Joe looks to find a way to build this city, he also feels defensive about his wife, probably because she was called his daughter by Amos Hicks. As they struggle to get a foothold in the community, Amos tries to interfere in their marriage but is quickly rebuked by Janie. Janie's loyalty is irrefutable; she had already shown her loyalty to Logan in a horrible situation, and the reader already can sense her loyalty to Joe. The reader will also sense in this chapter that the town's perspective is somewhat different from ours. Lee Coker sums up the town's feelings when he tells Hicks that he "can't take no 'oman lak dat from no man lak him." In short, the town shares the traditional point of view that the head of the household is the husband. In an isolated farm with Logan Killicks, it was easy for Janie to dismiss this point of view as unrealistic on Logan's part. It will be harder to dismiss when the entire town has this common view.

In fact, there is a dramatic change in the setting of the novel in this chapter. The Eatonville that we briefly saw in Chapter 1 is now presented to us as a complete picture. The reader will notice that the collective persona of the town described in the first chapter evolves here, and there can be no question that Joe Starks' success has a lot to do with the formation of the town's collective psyche. There is no doubt that Joe created a lot out of nothing in a very short time, and he is, at first, respected by everyone. As Joe becomes more and more successful, however, his ego is fed on the pride of the others. Their resentment is natural, but there is an additional hostility because Joe is a black man who acts in a way that they have only associated with white people. When Joe orders them around, they are pleased because the sense of accomplishment in building the town is shared by all. But as Joe becomes richer and richer, it seems as if the others are working for him without getting anything in return. They see Joe's possessions but are unable to share in them.

Furthermore, Joe is unwilling to share the glory with anyone, least of all his wife. Instead, his early success only causes him to be even more ambitious. When the first street lamp comes into town, Joe gives a speech about light. He says that "De Sun-maker brings it up in de mornin', and de Sun-maker sends it tuh bed at night," while "us poor weak humans can't do nothin' tuh hurry it up nor to

slow it down." However, he then provides the town with its own light, and while he downplays his role in the speech, the bombastic language implies that he is, in fact, calling himself a Sunmaker as well. He sees himself as the central figure in the town and becomes more egotistical as the town grows more resentful. As his ego grows, he feels the need to order everyone around, even Janie, which is what the townspeople complain about at the end of the chapter.

What hurts Janie the most is the fact that she is forgotten throughout all of this change. When the store is built, she is told to dress up because all of the other women in the town will be there, yet she is also kept quiet by Joe out of jealousy. Joe tells Janie she should be glad that he is mayor because that "makes uh big woman outa you." Janie's fear is justifiable; she has found out that she will remain in Joe's shadow and be called "Mrs. Mayor" instead of "Janie." Joe's wish to remain dominant has forced Janie to accept an even more limited social role than her role as Logan's wife. She cannot be a "normal" wife; she must be submissive and aloof in order to satisfy Joe's ambitions. While Janie is proud of him, she hasn't shared in his glory because he has kept all the glory for himself. Janie had thought that Joe's dreams would be modified to include her, but it seems that the dreams he had when he met her at the farm still only serve himself. What is worse for Janie is that Joe's abstract talk about dreams and desires has now become the talk of stores and street lamps. Janie finds out that Joe is the same sort of person as Logan, but the society Joe wishes to control is larger than one farm. Janie has now become one person out of an entire town that can help Joe. At least with Logan she was the only other worker, and therefore, could expect some attention.

The techniques Hurston uses in this chapter help the reader appreciate the difference in Janie's life. The most notable difference in this chapter is the replacement of Janie as the protagonist with Joe. The first half of this chapter focuses upon Joe and his struggle to build the town. Once he is in power, and the struggle is over, the focus still remains on Joe and the town. Where is Janie? This is a deliberate attempt by Hurston to show us the same discomfort that Janie must feel in this situation. After struggling with Janie and rejoicing over her escape from Logan, we wish to hear more about her and more from her. Instead, her role in the novel has been usurped by the imposing figure of Joe Starks. As we finish the chapter, we wish that Joe would be quiet, or that the townspeople who discuss Janie could find some sympathy for her. However, the reader is unable to control the situation. This is a direct parallel to Janie's plight, who has been silenced and is unable to do anything about it. The hope that the reader had at the beginning of the chapter is now gone, and the reader continues sympathizing with her and hoping against hope that the situation will improve.

Study Questions

1. What does Joe buy for Janie as they are traveling to Eatonville?

2. Describe the town as it is when Joe and Janie first arrive.

3. When Joe leaves town for the first time, who stays behind, and why?

4. How does Lee Coker respond to Amos Hicks and his criticism of Janie?

5. How does Hicks respond to Joe's announcement that he is going to get a post office for Eatonville?

6. Why is Tony Taylor upset at Lige Moss during the party celebrating the store's grand opening?

7. How does Joe decide to celebrate the arrival of the street lamp?

8. Describe the Starks' new house.

9. What did the phrase "Our beloved Mayor" mean to the residents of Eatonville?

10. Describe the incident between Henry Pitts and Joe Starks.

Answers

1. Joe bought Janie some apples and a candy dish that looked like a lantern.

2. When Janie and Joe first come to Eatonville, they are surprised to find it hardly a town at all. It is described in the novel as a "scant dozen of shame-faced houses scattered in the sand."

3. Amos Hicks stays behind in order to introduce himself to Janie and offer her any assistance she might need. Janie knows what sort of "assistance" Hicks means and politely refuses.

4. Lee Coker knows that Hicks is pretending that he doesn't like Janie only to make himself feel better after Janie rejected him.

5. Hicks laughs, saying that Starks is talking without doing anything. However, he feels a little nervous because he believes that Starks *can* get a post office, and "he wasn't ready to think of colored people in post offices yet."

6. Tony Taylor is mad because Lige Moss interrupts "the one speech of his lifetime," which was being made to welcome the Starks couple to Eatonville.

7. Joe arranges a barbecue to celebrate the town's first street lamp.

8. The Starks' house, which is called the "big house," is two stories high with porches and banisters. It is also painted bright white. All of the other houses look like "servants' quarters" when compared with the Starks' home.

9. According to the novel, the phrase "our beloved Mayor" is a phrase like "God is everywhere." Everybody says it but no one believes it.

10. Joe catches Henry Pitts trying to steal a load of his sugar cane and banishes him from the town. The other townspeople feel this is harsh because Starks was so wealthy and he didn't lose the load that Pitts was trying to take.

Suggested Essay Topics

1. Is Joe Starks an admirable man? Why or why not?

2. "He's de wind and we'se de grass. We bend which ever way he blows but at dat us needs him. De town wouldn't be nothin' if it wasn't for him." Sam Watson says that this is the relationship between Joe Starks and the town. Do you agree with Sam Watson? Why or why not?

Chapter 6

New Characters:

Matt Bonner: *An Eatonville resident who sells a mule that he mistreated to Joe Starks.*

Lige Moss and Walter Thomas: *Two men who pass time by sitting in front of the store and talking with Sam Watson.*

Hambo and Lum: *Two men who help out at Starks' store.*

Rev. and Mrs. Pearson: *Eatonville's pastor and his wife.*

Charlie Jones and Jim Weston: *Two men who compete for Daisy Blunt.*

Daisy Blunt: *A pretty young woman who lives in Eatonville.*

Mrs. Robbins: *A woman who always begs at Starks' store.*

Joe Lindsay and Jim Stone: *Two customers at Starks' store.*

Summary

Many years will pass in Chapter 6, and in these years Janie finds almost nothing except work in the store. Joe has forced her to tie up her hair in the store to keep the other men in the town from looking at her. It also seems as if Joe always asks Janie to help him in the store whenever there is a good story being told out on the store porch or something interesting is happening. Although most of the days are the same, there are a few incidents over the years that Janie remembers.

The first incident concerns Matt Bonner. His yellow mule is a constant source of ridicule for the men of the town, and Matt is usually the target of this ridicule. While it usually was in good-natured fun, several men start to tease the mule when it wanders by the store one day. Janie looks at this cruelty and mutters to herself about how horrible they are for hurting that wretched creature. Joe hears her and calls Matt Bonner into the store. Matt Bonner sells Joe the mule for five dollars and then boasts that the mule is worked out and will probably die soon. However, Joe tells Matt that he bought the mule so that it could rest, not work. This act is looked upon with awe, and Joe earns the respect of the townspeople for it.

Janie is so moved that she makes a speech, which surprises the townspeople. The yellow mule becomes a beloved mascot and the center of many tall tales told around the store.

While Janie would like to share in the tales and talk that goes around the store, Joe keeps her from joining in conversations by giving her a task to do in the store. Joe continually puts down Sam Watson and Lige Moss as people who do nothing but talk all day. Janie notices that Joe seems to enjoy their endless bickering even though he never directly participates. Another time, the single men start buying things in the store to impress Daisy Blunt and start arguing with each other. Janie is having a good laugh until Joe reprimands her in front of everybody else for supposedly missing an order.

These subtle but constant put-downs wear Janie down and she talks less and less in order not to create a scene. As time passes, Janie understands that Joe Starks is not the man she should have married. Nevertheless, she continues to fight, knowing that it is useless because the more she talks, the harder Joe tries to keep her quiet. One night, for the first time, Joe slaps Janie after she accidentally ruins dinner. Janie looks into herself and realizes that she is waiting for someone else.

That same night, after she changes her clothes, she heads down to the store, where she finds Joe joking with Mrs. Robbins. Joe wants to apologize but doesn't know how, so he tries to create a playful atmosphere at Mrs. Robbins' expense. Mrs. Robbins always begs at Joe's store even though her husband pays for everything. Joe humors her, because her husband has asked him to, but later joins the men in poking fun at her. When the talk turns to derision of women in general, Janie quickly observes the faults of men and is just as quickly made quiet by Joe. The opportunity of a reconciliation lost, Janie becomes more quiet, and Joe ignores her in order to force an apology.

Analysis

The tone of this chapter is decidedly less optimistic than the previous chapters. With Joe's power established, the excitement that came with the rapid changes of the town is now gone. The surroundings are vividly described and the anecdotes are wonderful,

but throughout these entertaining yarns the reader notices above all that Janie is absent from them. When we read about Janie, we usually see her eager to join in, like a child looking through a fence at a game. The reader's enjoyment is dampened by Janie's presence, because without her participation, the reader too feels like an outsider.

In this chapter, we also receive serious insight to Joe's character. We already knew that he was a savvy businessman. His attitude towards the townspeople is more of a mystery. He projects an outgoing personality to the townspeople but secretly feels superior to them. He is capable of good things, but he is an insecure man who surrounds himself with property and power to compensate. When he doesn't feel threatened, he can be very magnanimous, especially if that generosity benefits him as well. The case with Matt Bonner's mule is an example of his complex character.

The mule had always been a joke among the townspeople, and would have probably been teased to death if it were not for Joe's interference. Janie identifies with the mule, because it is at the mercy of people and helpless on its own. The mule has been weakened with constant abuse, but cannot fight back due to the constant pressure to which he has been subjected. Joe's purchase of the mule is a very kind act that we didn't expect. There are two ironic aspects of Joe's purchase. The first is that Joe earns the respect of the town, who likens the freeing of the mule to the freeing of a slave. Only Joe could have done this without ridicule, due to his position. The others would never have thought of letting the mule rest, not because they are cruel, but because they follow a collective morality which allows them to be cruel without responsibility. If one of them had decided to act morally on his own, however, he would probably have been teased as well. Joe's power allows him to break away from the town psychology and act on his own.

The true irony, however, is that Joe makes this decision only after seeing Janie's outrage at the abuse of the mule. While Joe proves he has the ability to perform kind acts, Janie's influence on him shows the reader that he doesn't have the inclination to be kind on his own. Janie has this moral character but does not have the power to implement her will anymore except through Joe. Her situation is similar to the mule because she must also look to someone in power to "free" her. Janie's speech afterwards shows some hope; if Joe is praised for kindness, perhaps he will be able to show more kindness in the future. Unfortunately, this will be a rare case. Joe cannot get any benefit from freeing Janie, so he continues to keep her under his control.

He prizes above all, his position in Eatonville, and it seems that when his position of power is threatened, he will resort to oppression and violence. To him, Janie is more of a possession than a wife, and her purpose is to support him as he performs his duties as mayor and store owner. When Janie attempts to assert her independence, it is seen by Joe as a threat to his power. He attempts to control Janie with mental and physical abuse, not because he truly wishes to hurt her, but because he feels it is necessary to maintain his aura of power. Even when he hits her, he feels guilty, but would only be able to apologize "on his own terms," that is, without a loss of face.

Due to Joe's understanding of the social atmosphere, he cannot maintain an even relationship with Janie because that would be seen as a sign of weakness in the town. The wife is seen as an underling in Eatonville, and Janie, as the mayor's wife, is public figure. This is the justification Joe uses for himself whenever he orders Janie around in public or humiliates her in front of everybody. He feels that to treat Janie equally will expose him to ridicule from the people in the store. This probably wouldn't be the case, of course. There is a very humorous scene in the novel which illustrates the power women can hold over men. When Daisy Blunt enters the store, several men proceed to make fools out of themselves and each other for her sake. The perception that the husband is the head of the family, however, is too strong a tradition for Joe to consider breaking.

His ridicule of Mrs. Robbins is another example of this cowardice. Mrs. Robbins is a vulnerable target, much like the mule, due to her mental instability and her position as a wife. The people of the town, including Joe, not only make fun of her but also make fun of her husband's devotion to her. Joe Lindsay looks upon Mr. Robbins' refusal to beat her "with scornful disapproval." After hearing this, Janie does "what she had never done before, thrust herself into the conversation" because she cannot stand the injustice of these words. This time, she takes the moral stance without protection from her powerful husband. Indeed, Joe immediately quiets her, proving once again that while Joe holds land and property, Janie is the one moral superior in the town.

After Joe hits her, Janie realizes that Joe was never the right man for her. Her image of Joe falls "off the shelf inside her." When she examines this image, she understands that he was "just something she had grabbed up to drape her dreams over." It was something different from Logan that she had wanted, not Joe himself. Now, she wants something different from Joe but is already trapped by her obligation to her marriage. She had defended herself against this oppression by closing her "blossomy openings dusting pollen" to Joe. She can no longer be her "natural" self to Joe. She now understands that she was "saving up feelings for some man she had never seen." Her situation is very bleak by the end of this chapter, because she has now admitted to herself that Joe will never change.

Study Questions

1. Sam tells Matt that his mule is in trouble by the lake. What has supposedly happened with the mule?

2. What does Joe do before he buys the mule?

3. How much does Matt get for the mule?

4. What is Sam and Lige's argument about?

5. What position does each man hold in this argument, and what proof do they offer?

6. Why are Jim and Dave arguing in the store?

7. How does Joe ruin the argument for Janie?

8. According to Joe, what is the difference between him and Janie?

9. Why does Joe pretend to read the paper when Mrs. Robbins walks in?

10. What does God supposedly tell Janie?

Answers

1. The women of the town are washing clothes by the lake and are using the mule's ribs for a washboard.

2. Joe changes his shoes in order to make Matt wait longer.

3. Matt sells his mule for five dollars.

4. Lige asks Sam if it is caution or nature that keeps a man from sitting on a stove.

5. Lige maintains that caution keeps a man from touching a stove because you have to teach babies not to touch stoves. Therefore, caution is taught and not natural. Sam believes that at the root of everything is nature, and since nature created caution, nature is what keeps a man from hurting himself.

6. They are arguing about who loves Daisy Blunt more.

7. Janie is watching the argument with pleasure, but Joe calls her into the store to wait on Mrs. Bogle.

8. Joe claims that their difference is "When Ah sees one thing Ah understands ten. You see ten things and don't understand one." In other words, Janie needs him to work properly, but he doesn't need her.

9. Everyone in the store is waiting for Mrs. Robbins to plead. Once she does, everyone laughs and Joe begins to humor her.

10. God tells Janie that men will be surprised if they "ever find out you don't know half as much" about women as they think.

Suggested Essay Topics

1. Could all of the fighting between Joe and Janie have been avoided? Do you think that Janie could ever be happy with Joe as her husband?

2. How would you interpret the scene of the buzzards?

Chapter 7

New Character:

Steve Mixon: *A customer who buys tobacco at the Starks' store.*

Summary

Time passes in the same manner as Chapter 6, and Janie finds herself unsatisfied with the way Joe treats her but is resigned to it. Occasionally she fantasizes about going away again but dismisses the idea because she is 35 years old now. She still feels the need to support him because if he isn't anybody special "life won't be nothin' but uh store and uh house."

Joe has become an old man, and knows it himself. Joe starts to comment about Janie's age and appearance, thinking that it will deflect attention about his own age. One day Janie makes a mistake in the store, which allows Joe to insult her in front of some customers. Janie has had all she can take, and tells him that "when you pull down yo' britches, you look like da change uh life." After she finishes, the customers start to tease Joe, and Joe realizes they don't respect him anymore. Joe can't deal with this, and can do nothing to retaliate except hit Janie and kick her out of the store.

Analysis

While the preceding chapter established the relationship between Janie and Joe is an unequal and unhappy one, this chapter explores the tragic elements of this relationship. Janie has dealt with her unhappiness by numbing herself to the pain. She reverts to the same sort of daydreaming that she used to hide herself from Logan. While she still had some hope of escaping Logan's marriage, and therefore a reason to daydream, now her dreams are nothing more than distant wishes. The years she has spent married to Joe have affected her self-esteem; she thinks of herself as an older woman and can see Joe has become an old man. Janie has considered that Joe probably is not the great man he has considered himself, but nonetheless, tells herself "he's got tuh be else Ah ain't got nothin' to live for." These years have linked Janie's destiny with Joe, and she now feels obligated to stay in this marriage until its end.

Chapter 6 had chronicled the slow wearing down of their relationship; in this chapter the reader witnesses the breakdown. Joe had built for himself a small empire, which was the only place in which he felt secure. Over the years, he had grown accustomed to imposing his will on others, and first and foremost, Janie. Now he has become aware of his own mortality with his advanced age. This has deeply shocked him, because he had become used to his power. Now, he feels the need to assert himself even more, and he compensates by abusing Janie. However, his insults about Janie's age do not fool anybody, least of all her. Janie "saw he was hurting inside so she let it pass without comment," knowing that he was going through a terrible time. Joe has never confided his fears to his wife, so Janie helps him in the only way she can, by permitting him to make fun of her.

This understanding is destroyed when Joe humiliates her in public. Joe takes advantage of their unspoken agreement, and destroys the sympathy that Janie (and the reader) had felt for him.

The previous two chapters in the novel have been peppered with many interesting and humorous arguments. In this town and culture, arguing plays an important social role, with each participant battling as if in a duel to outdo the other. Since there is a lot of honor involved, there seem to be unwritten rules as well. In the arguments of Chapters 5 and 6 (Coker/Hicks, Sam Wilson/Lige Moss, and Jim/Dave over Daisy), the goal was to prove a point or to get a laugh from the audience. Even the teasing of Matt Bonner is only slightly mean-spirited. Joe's comments are just plain cruel, in a feeble attempt to distract the town from his rapid aging. Since he steps over the line, Janie retaliates in stunning fashion, and with a few sentences, she "had robbed him of his illusion." Joe can see for the first time in his life that he is a source of amusement. The townspeople, perhaps still slightly resentful of Joe's position, don't hesitate to rub it in. Hurston states it succinctly: "When he paraded his possessions hereafter, they would not consider the two together. They'd look with envy at the things and pity the man that owned him."

Joe learns that his position of power is directly connected to his wealth, which is a tremendous blow to his ego. Joe's reaction to this revelation is not unexpected. He cannot do anything except

lash out now that his self-perception has been shattered. But this does not accomplish anything and is clearly the beginning of the end for he and Janie together.

Study Questions

1. What did Janie get from Joe?
2. Explain the following sentence. "She sat and watched the shadow of herself going about tending store and prostrating itself before Jody, while all the time she herself sat under a shady tree with the wind blowing through her hair and her clothes."
3. Why does Joe tell Janie to stop playing croquet?
4. How does Joe look older?
5. What mistake does Janie make in the store?
6. Why do people stop laughing at Joe's insult of Janie's body?
7. According to Janie, what has Joe "mixed up"?
8. How does Janie describe herself to Joe?
9. Who starts to tease Joe after Janie's retort?
10. What does "playin' de dozens" mean?

Answers

1. According to the novel, "she got nothing from Jody except what money could buy."
2. Janie had withdrawn into herself so deeply that she now daydreams even when she talks with Joe and works around the store.
3. Joe tells Janie to stop playing because she will allegedly become so sore she won't be able to get out of bed tomorrow.
4. Instead of sitting in a chair, Joe now just falls into it. His eyes are missing a little spark of life, and his belly, which was always prominent, now "sagged like a load suspended from his loins."
5. The piece of tobacco that she cuts for Steve Mixon is too big.

6. They are a little ashamed of themselves after the impact of Joe's insult is understood. There is nothing good-natured in Joe's words; the customers are used to laughing at harmless teasing but this is clearly not the case here.

7. Joe has confused what Janie did with what Janie looks like.

8. Janie says that she looks her age, which means that she is a mature woman and not an old maid.

9. Walter and Lige Moss start to taunt Joe.

10. The "dozens" is a term used when two people have an exchange of insults in front of others. This style of verbal fighting is especially prominent in black American culture. The aim is to display verbal ability, as well as insult in a good natured way.

Suggested Essay Topics

1. Describe the argument between Joe and Janie as if you were a customer in the store who witnessed the entire scene. Try to use the point of view of a person from Eatonville, not your own.

2. Why didn't Janie walk away? (This is not as easy a question as it seems. Try to understand Janie's position.)

Chapter 8

New Character:

Pheoby Watson: *Janie's best friend and Sam Watson's wife.*

Summary

Immediately after the scene in Chapter 7, Joe moves out of the bedroom in their house. They seldom talk to each other now. In spite of everything, Janie still wants Joe to be on good terms with her but knows by now that her words cannot make him reasonable. She takes his silence philosophically and waits for him to "get over his mad spell."

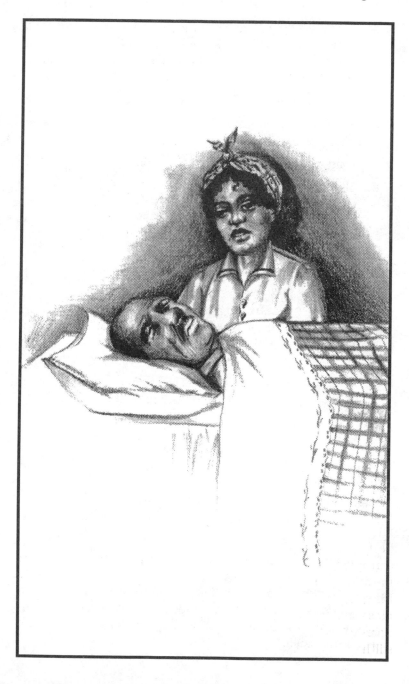

Joe's health continues to fail him. As he takes to bed, he becomes more sullen and refuses to see Janie. It seems that everyone can now visit Joe except her. Janie is terribly hurt by his isolation and tries to get her friends to convince him to change his mind. Janie learns from Pheoby Watson that a rumor has been going around town that she has cursed him. This rumor was started by a medicine man who has now become Joe's friend. Joe is relying on medicine men to cure him, but everybody knows that it is only a matter of time. Janie is beside herself when she hears news from Sam Watson and uses him to get a real doctor to Jody. The doctor tells her that it is just a matter of time.

Determined to see him one last time, Janie finally forces herself into Joe's room to talk with him. Joe wants nothing to do with her, but Janie talks anyway. Joe remains insolent until Janie tells him that he will die soon. Joe doesn't want to hear this but Janie finally has his attention and continues. Janie wishes that things could have been different, but it is all too painful for Joe to hear now. He orders her out but Janie isn't finished; as she tells him that his insults and control "ain't whut Ah rushed off down de road tuh find out about you," a sound emanates from Joe's throat and he dies.

As Janie looks at Joe lying dead, she feels pity for him "for the first time in years." Janie takes a long look in her mirror and removes the kerchief that Joe always made her wear. After she combs her hair and ties it back up, she goes out to announce her husband's death to the town.

Analysis

Joe and Janie's marriage finally ends in the chapter, as does their conflict. Joe's revelation from the last chapter, that he is no longer the figure of power that he has always pictured himself to be, has deeply affected him. As he becomes sicker and sicker, he surrounds himself in denial. He is desperate to think of himself as the same strong man who built Eatonville. In doing so, he feeds his ego by talking to anyone who is willing to listen. The charlatans who are welcomed by Joe clearly want his wealth, but Joe ignores this due to his vulnerable state. In the previous chapter, Joe still had enough pride to be hurt when he found out that his wealth was more valued than his character in Eatonville, but now even this pride is gone. Joe also deliberately ignores Janie in order to prove his superiority. He invites in townspeople who would have never been allowed in before "unless it were to do some menial job." Joe trades in the respect that the townspeople had for him in order to prove to Janie that he is still a beloved and important man.

Janie is hurt deeply from being ignored and distrusted. Joe expertly utilizes the town psychology in order to ostracize her from the rest of the town. Pheoby Watson tries to comfort Janie, but it is difficult when the entire town seems to be against her. Even though no one truly believes the rumor that she is the cause of Joe's sickness, the awe that they hold for Joe is too hard to break. Joe is providing them with the opportunity to be his confidants, and they keep his trust by telling him what his wife is doing. Joe sets Janie apart by continuing to portray her as his enemy, who is therefore the enemy of his new "friends." It is his last opportunity to exert control before his inevitable death.

The personification of death in this chapter provides a contrast to Joe's imagined power and true weakness. He thought that his property made him a big man, but even though he is still the biggest landowner in Eatonville, the description of his appearance is certainly not respectful. Janie sees Joe becoming "baggy" and weak, but his stubbornness becomes even stronger. The belief that he can cheat death is the height of his ego, and, ironically, the cause of his death. He refuses to see a doctor and simply blames his ill health on Janie, a convenient scapegoat, rather than admit he needs help from others.

Janie's last words to Joe are not welcomed, because her gift is the one thing he never had or needed in his life: honesty. Janie gives him the painful truth, not only the fact that he will die soon, but also a true portrait of his character. Janie's truthful words are neither spiteful nor the grand assertion that the reader was probably hoping for. Janie doesn't look for revenge; she simply attempts to express to Joe the regret that she feels over these years.

Janie looks at Joe's death with a mixture of sorrow and relief. Her parting words to him represent the waste and the unhappiness of unmet expectations. His departure is sad, but with his death comes a new beginning, symbolized by Janie's removal of her hair rag. As she combs her hair and looks at herself in the mirror, the reader knows that she is looking forward to another change in her life. She puts the rag back on, however, because she still must play the role of Jody Starks' widow, and to do so, she must be "just what people wanted to see." But there can be no doubt that with Joe dead, his suppression of her is dead as well.

Study Questions

1. Where does Joe sleep after the fight from the preceding chapter?

2. Explain the following sentence: "Well, if she must eat out of a long-handled spoon, she must."

3. Since Joe is refusing to see Janie, who is cooking and cleaning for him?

4. What does Pheoby advise Janie to do about the rumor that she is poisoning her husband?

5. What does Pheoby know about the medicine man who started the rumor about Janie?

6. What medical problem does Joe have?

7. Describe the character of Death.

8. Joe claims that Janie never had sympathy for him. Does Janie agree?

9. What does Janie want Joe to do before he dies?

10. What has been waiting for Janie in the looking glass?

Answers

1. Joe moves his things to a room downstairs and sleeps there.

2. It means that Janie cannot do anything to change her situation, so she must live with it.

3. Old lady Davis is doing the housechores, even though Janie is a better cook.

4. Pheoby tells Janie to act as if she doesn't know about the rumor and to say nothing about it, since nobody believes it anyway.

5. That same man tried to sell gophers last year to people in Eatonville.

6. Joe's kidneys have failed.

7. Death is described in the novel as "that strange being with the huge square toes who lived way in the West. The great one who lived in the straight house like a platform without sides to it, and without a roof." In the legend, he waits for a messenger to call him to come.

8. Janie had a lot of sympathy, but she tells Joe "ah just didn't never git no chance tuh use none of it."

9. Janie wants him to listen to what she has to say.

10. Janie's "girl self" has been waiting for her in the looking glass.

Suggested Essay Topics

1. Is it too late to feel sorry for Joe? Why or why not?

2. Read Joe and Janie's final conversation once again. Examine Joe's words and comment on his mentality. Why is he so unforgiving to her?

Chapter 9

New Character:

Ike Green: *One of the many men who tries to marry Janie after Joe's death.*

Summary

Chapter 9 begins with Joe's funeral, which is described as "the finest thing Orange County had ever seen with Negro eyes." Janie attends the funeral and appears somber and unhappy, but she is still hiding her true emotions. Inside, she is preparing for her new life, which she begins by burning all the head rags she wore and wearing her hair in a braid that hangs below her waist.

She continues to run the store but slowly lets Hezekiah adopt the duties that Joe used to do. She has no interest in the store and contemplates her next move. She thinks about returning to her grandmother's resting place and trying to locate her mother but ultimately decides against it. She discovers that neither one of them really interests her anymore.

Janie also discovers that as a rich widow she finds herself with a lot more visitors than she used to have. Men of all ages come to the store to tell her that "uh woman by herself is uh pitiful thing," and to offer to help in taking care of business. Janie ignores them and confesses to Pheoby that she loves being alone right now. When Pheoby warns her that the town would think she isn't showing respect to Joe, Janie replies that "mourning oughtn't tuh last no longer'n grief."

Analysis

This chapter has a sense of hope that was lacking in the previous chapters. Joe's death has liberated Janie, and with this freedom Janie has become less irritable and less sensitive. Joe's death allows the town to forget about his shortcomings and focus upon his accomplishments, which is the sort of way Joe always wanted to be idolized while he was alive. Janie, however, is still alive, and the town expects her to fulfill her stereotypical role as the mourning widow. Since this is a much less painful role for Janie, she easily meets the town's expectations. She also continues to work at the store and to play the part of Joe Starks' wife, but now without Joe's abuse. Her work becomes more satisfying with the knowledge that she can leave at any time.

Janie uses her free time to reflect upon her past. She discovers that she hated Nanny and the way she had lived but "had hidden it from herself all these years under a cloak of pity." Janie had never had any use for Nanny's idea of security. It was this security that caused Janie to marry Logan in the first place. This safety was also very restrictive to Janie, but she had never realized that until now. Her hatred of Nanny comes from her belief that Janie should have been secure. Janie discovers that her perspective of life didn't focus on possessions and security; she "had been getting ready for her great journey to the horizons in search of people." To her, someone who worries about things and possessions is someone who "loved to deal in scraps." Janie's vision of life was always bigger than this, but "she had been whipped like a cur dog" until she had changed her vision to satisfy her husband. The implication is that she will no longer be whipped.

Because her life has suddenly been liberated, she now finds the town more humorous than oppressive. The men of the town show their ignorance and sexism by courting Janie so soon after Joe's death. Janie's moral character is so different from the rest of the town that it is simple for her to see the true intentions of Ike Green and all the rest. When the women come to pay her a visit, they hold her to a higher standard, and are very "respectful and stiff" with her. Janie, on the other hand, would rather go fishing with Pheoby Watson. The town, which had been in awe of Joe and finds his death tragic, still thinks of Janie as Joe's woman. The respect she gets has been based upon her previous identity. But Janie doesn't care about that identity anymore and is too happy with her new-found freedom to let the shallow perspective of the townspeople affect her.

One more image is profound in this chapter. The image of the horizon is used as a symbol for the grandness of life, the type of life Janie wants to pursue. Nanny's view of life reduced everything to a meager possession or item; she took the infinite horizon "and pinched it in to such a little bit of a thing that she could tie it around her granddaughter's neck tight enough to choke her." Janie wants to live with a grand vision, and the horizon becomes that vision.

Study Questions

1. What song does the Elks band play during Joe's funeral?

2. Why is Janie content to keep things as they are for now?

3. What does Janie do during the evenings?

4. Why does Janie consider returning to where she came from?

5. How long has Joe been dead when Ike Green proposes to help Janie?

6. How does Janie get rid of Ike Green?

7. How long does Janie wear black?

8. How does Hezekiah become more like Joe?

9. How do the townspeople treat Janie after she starts to wear white?

10. Who is pressuring Pheoby to introduce him to Janie?

Answers

1. The band plays the song "Safe in the Arms of Jesus."

2. Janie knows that she has the rest of her life to live as she wants, and there is no need to rush into her new life.

3. She lets Hezekiah tend the store during the evenings while she sits on the porch.

4. She thinks she might want to take care of Nanny's grave and "look over the old stomping ground."

5. Joe has been dead less than two months when Ike Green visits her.

6. Janie excuses herself, saying that she needs to help Hezekiah with a barrel of sugar. Once she gets inside the store, she tells Hezekiah that she is going home and that he should let her know when Ike Green is gone.

7. Janie wears black clothes for six months.

8. Hezekiah starts to smoke cigars and adopts some of Joe's old sayings.

9. They visit Janie often but are very polite. She is treated with respect, though she is never able to talk on a personal level with anyone except Pheoby Watson.

10. An undertaker from Sanford was hoping Pheoby could introduce him to Janie.

Suggested Essay Topics

1. What do you feel is more valued in our society, personal relationships or material wealth? Are the values in our society any different from those in Eatonville?

2. How does the tradition of mourning affect Janie's life? Comment on the town's expectations of her.

Chapter 10

New Character:

Tea Cake (Vergible) Woods: *A fun-loving man who lives a few miles from Eatonville.*

Summary

Janie is alone in the store one day because the rest of the town, including Hezekiah, is in Winter Park watching a baseball game. Since no one has come to the store, Janie decides to close up early. Just then, Tea Cake Woods walks into the store, and explains that he thought the game was at a different park. Janie and Tea Cake immediately trade jokes, and Tea Cake teaches her how to play checkers.

Tea Cake pretends to leave, but ends up staying until late in the evening, joking with her and the other customers who have walked in from the finished ball game. As Janie closes up the store, Tea Cake offers to walk her home. Janie accepts, and as Tea Cake leaves, Janie is struck with the feeling "as if she had known him all her life."

Analysis

Tea Cake makes his first appearance in the novel. Just as Joe Starks first appeared in the novel, Tea Cake makes an immediate impression on Janie. When Janie was a young girl, she was stricken by Joe's appearance, which she had never seen before. Janie's first impression of Tea Cake takes place on an emotional level. The smile that is on Tea Cake's face makes Janie want to laugh before she even talks to him. This introduction is also pleasant to the reader, since the light tone is a marked contrast to the intense situations presented during her marriage with Joe.

The difference in Tea Cake's behavior with Janie is also a contrast to Joe's opinion of her. Tea Cake is surprised that Janie doesn't know how to play checkers. Janie had never learned because Joe had said "it wuz too heavy fuh [her] brains." Tea Cake obviously doesn't believe this nonsense, the very thing which Joe had been telling her so often that Janie had started to believe it herself. Janie

has become so used to her accepted role that the very fact that "somebody wanted her to play" was a welcome change. Not only does he teach her, but he doesn't insult her intelligence by letting her win. This is her first relationship with a man that is based on mutual respect, and it is established from their first meeting. Due to his immediate impact, the reader understands that Tea Cake will play a major role in later chapters.

Study Questions

1. At what time does Tea Cake come into the store?
2. What does Tea Cake buy at the store?
3. Does Janie like checkers?
4. Why does Janie complain about their game?
5. How does Tea Cake intend to get home?
6. Why didn't Tea Cake tell Janie his name until she asks for it?
7. How does Janie joke about his nickname?
8. What is "knuckle puddin'"?
9. What name does Janie call Tea Cake, and how does he like this name?
10. What does Janie do after Tea Cake walks away?

Answers

1. Tea Cake comes into the store at five-thirty.
2. Tea Cake buys a pack of cigarettes.
3. Janie doesn't know if she likes checkers or not because she has never played before.
4. Tea Cake had jumped Janie's king, and Janie complains that she wasn't paying attention.
5. He will hop a train if there are any trains still running, or he will simply walk the seven miles to his home.
6. Tea Cake says he didn't expect to use his name in the store today.

7. She wonders if Tea Cake is as sweet as his nickname.

8. "Knuckle puddin'" is a beating with the fist. Tea Cake asks Janie if he could buy some as a joke.

9. Janie calls him "Mr. Tea Cake," and he tells her that she can be polite and call him "Mr. Woods," or be friendly and call him "Tea Cake." He would prefer her to be friendly.

10. Janie sits on her porch and watches the moon rise.

Suggested Essay Topics

1. Do you think this is "love at first sight"? Should Janie be cautious after two failed relationships? Write a paragraph as if you were Janie's friend and she asks you for advice concerning Tea Cake.

2. How does Hurston use humor in this chapter? Contrast this humor with the "dozens" in previous chapters.

Chapter 11

Summary

A week has passed since Janie's first meeting with Tea Cake, and Janie has made up her mind not to pay any attention to him if she should see him again. Once he comes in, however, she can't help but join in the fun. They spend the day laughing and playing checkers and end up spending the entire night fishing by the lake. The next day, Hezekiah offers to take her home and warns her against Tea Cake, even though he doesn't have a reputation for being wicked or violent.

Tea Cake shows up at Janie's house the following night with some fish. After dinner, Tea Cake starts to sing and puts Janie to sleep. Janie wakes up and finds Tea Cake combing her hair. As he compliments her appearance, Janie gets up to go to bed. Tea Cake feels that she is saying this just to get rid of him and tells her that he feels special with her. Janie wants to believe him but cannot bring herself to do so. Tea Cake leaves, but Janie looks at herself in the mirror for a long time before she goes to bed.

Janie simply cannot stop thinking about him. When he returns again in two days, they have dinner and spend the night together. Janie feels wonderful with him but is still plagued with doubt. When Tea Cake invites her to a Sunday School picnic, Janie gives him a chance to take back his invitation, thinking that he was just being polite. But Tea Cake insists upon taking her. Janie begs him not to lie to her, and Tea Cake says to her, "nobody else on earth kin hold uh candle to yuh, baby. You got de keys to de kingdom."

Analysis

The relationship between Tea Cake and Janie develops further in this chapter. Their feelings obviously grow deeper, and their mutual attraction becomes noticeable. Janie starts to feel something that she hasn't felt for years. These rekindled emotions, however, come in conflict with her habitual surroundings. She has lived in an area where her identity has been established for years. Her romance with Tea Cake contradicts this identity, and as a result, causes Janie to second-guess what she is doing.

Janie's doubt is caused by many different things. The most prominent cause in this chapter is her self-doubt, brought about by the fact that she is 12 years older than he is and is exacerbated by the mentality of the town. When she and Tea Cake go fishing, Janie makes him leave by the back gate, as if there were "some great secret she was keeping from the town." Hezekiah feels no qualms about interfering for her sake; her position as the richest widow in the town has already made her the target of the men. Hezekiah warns her but cannot disparage Tea Cake in any way except to say that he is poor. There are stereotypes of relationships ingrained into the town; a younger, poorer man with an older, richer woman is a type of relationship so unusual that it becomes immediate fodder for the gossip hounds. In such a case, the townspeople will have already assumed that the poorer person instigated the relationship in order to get money. Even though Janie might not believe it herself, she does have some subconscious doubts from these stereotypes. Tea Cake can sense that she might be thinking he has an ulterior motive, and tries hard to convince her that it is not true.

The language of the novel is also ambivalent; if we go back to Chapter 4, when Janie decided to run off with Joe, we read that Joe is "a bee for her bloom." Janie was confident that she had married something better than Logan, and used her favorite ideas to make the marriage seem like a dream come true. Tea Cake has now caused Janie to think about flowers and trees once again, which are symbols of innocent love for her. However, the narrator says that Tea Cake "could be a bee to a blossom." Why is there uncertainty now? Janie's experience with Logan and Joe has made her wary of men. The pleasure she had from being alone doesn't compare to the pleasure she has with Tea Cake, but with this pleasure comes a sizable risk of being made a fool. After being told for 20 years that she is old and doesn't know anything, Janie doesn't have the confidence to run off and leave everything she did with Joe. She wants to be convinced with tangible proof, rather than her feelings. After having to live through one failed dream, she doesn't want to experience failure again.

Hurston's use of symbols in this chapter reminds the reader of Janie's dreams and youth. Janie laughs more in this chapter than in all of the previous chapters during her other marriages. We can see some of her dreams fulfilled; instead of wistfully minding the store while the others are having fun, Janie joins in the fun. The town is surprised seeing her playing checkers, but welcomes her into the group. These longings had gone unfulfilled for so long that a checker game has a significant impact upon her and the reader. Janie also starts to become aware of her beauty. Her hair, which had been kept off limits by Joe, is now made an object of desire once again. Joe had been jealous when others had looked at her beautiful hair, so he ordered it covered to assert possession over it, and her. Now, Tea Cake strokes her hair, which allows them both to have pleasure. Janie's implied permission to Tea Cake is not only a sign that Janie has feelings for him, but also the release of a suppressed desire. What Janie wanted from Joe during their marriage she now finds in Tea Cake.

Study Questions

1. Why does Tea Cake tell Janie to have another Coca-Cola?

2. Where do Janie and Tea Cake go fishing?

3. How is Tea Cake prepared to play with Janie's hair?

4. What kind of fish does Tea Cake catch for Janie?

5. What does Janie wish about herself?

6. How much does Tea Cake want to bet Janie that he loves her?

7. Why does Tea Cake wake Janie up a couple of days after their fight?

8. What is Tea Cake doing in Janie's hammock?

9. Why does Tea Cake bring a car to Janie's store?

10. How long has Tea Cake been saving money to take Janie to the picnic?

Answers

1. Janie had her first soda alone, and "it wasn't done right dat time."

2. They go fishing at Lake Sabelia.

3. He brought a comb in case he had an opportunity to comb her hair that night.

4. Tea Cake catches some trout.

5. Janie wishes that she could be 12 years younger.

6. Tea Cake wants to bet a dollar, but then says that Janie has probably never made a bet in her life.

7. Tea Cake wants to prove to Janie that his feelings during the day are as honest as his feelings at night.

8. Tea Cake is pretending to be asleep.

9. Tea Cake wants to travel to a larger grocery store in order to buy things for the picnic.

10. Tea Cake has been saving money for two weeks.

Suggested Essay Topics

1. Why does Hezekiah find it necessary to interfere on Janie's behalf? Discuss his behavior and look to previous chapters to explain his motivation.

2. Is Tea Cake being deliberately mysterious? Discuss his nature and his theatrics.

Chapter 12

Summary

The town becomes a little disturbed after they see Tea Cake and Janie together at the picnic. After their first appearance together in a place other than the store, it seems like Tea Cake and Janie can be seen together everywhere. Rumors start to fly around town, and all of the townspeople believe that Tea Cake is trying to swindle Janie out of her money. These rumors reach Sam Watson, who discusses these rumors with his wife, Pheoby. Pheoby dismisses them as jealousy, but is concerned about Janie and what she is doing. She makes up her mind to see Janie to find out what is going on.

Janie tells Pheoby that she and Tea Cake plan to get married and leave Eatonville. Pheoby is wary of this and asks Janie gently if she is sure she is doing the right thing. Janie assures Pheoby and says "if people thinks de same they can make it all right." Janie wants to live her own life and swears Pheoby to secrecy.

Analysis

Tea Cake and Janie make their relationship public in Eatonville, which immediately becomes the hot topic of conversation. Hurston makes effective use of the narrator to illustrate the sort of talk that goes on behind Janie's back. The first paragraph is written as if it is the collective voice of the town, with every sentence either denouncing Janie and Tea Cake or expressing sympathy for Joe. People believe that Janie is not showing the proper respect for Joe, even though half of these people have already propositioned her. The town finds a lot of reasons to be annoyed with their going out together. In their code of moral behavior, such behavior is not acceptable. Janie is held to a more difficult standard because of her position as the widow of Joe Starks.

Eventually the talk reaches the Watsons, who hold a special place in the town because of Pheoby's relationship with Janie. Sam Watson repeats some of the standard rumors, but his motivation is concern for Janie rather than jealousy. Sam also took the unpopular stance in Chapter 5, supporting Joe when public opinion was against him. He has shown himself to be a man strong enough to speak his own mind, so the reader can interpret his concern for Janie as genuine. Pheoby is in a more difficult position; as Janie's closest friend, she also becomes a source from which the others attempt to gain information. Pheoby Watson is perceptive enough to know that the rumors are based on jealousy, but nonetheless, believes some of these rumors herself. When she talks with Janie and learns of her plans to marry, Pheoby is torn between the town's moral code and her duty to Janie as a friend.

Janie has a very difficult time breaking her accepted role in society. Joe's forced isolation of her caused Janie to miss many of the events in the town. The townspeople never knew that it wasn't Janie's free choice. Even Pheoby says that Janie "always did class off," and Tea Cake's activities with Janie are misinterpreted as "draggin' [Janie] round tuh places [she] ain't used to." This is a difficult role for Janie to break because it means breaking a stereotype that the entire town is used to believing.

Janie's decision to marry Tea Cake successfully frees her from Joe's prison of obligation and mental anguish. Her youthful innocence that caused her to leave with Joe has returned. She has enough faith in Tea Cake to once again risk the unknown. The gossip in the town doesn't affect her because she has left their way of life. She is making the same transition she made when she left with Joe, hoping to find some sort of pleasure.

Study Questions

1. How long has Joe been dead in this chapter?

2. What color does Janie usually wear?

3. What does the Pastor say about Tea Cake?

4. Where does Pheoby stop before she goes to Janie's house?

5. Why doesn't Janie wear mourning clothes anymore?

6. Why is Pheoby scared that Janie is becoming like a possum?

7. Why does Janie decide to sell the store?

8. What does Janie mean when she says, "ah done lived Grandma's way, now ah means to live mine"?

9. How is Pheoby like a chicken?

10.   What costume is Janie preparing for her marriage to Tea Cake?

Answers

1.   Joe has been dead less than nine months at the beginning of the chapter.

2.   Janie usually wears blue clothes now.

3.   The Pastor says that Tea Cake has been keeping Janie from attending church.

4.   Pheoby stopped at other houses before she goes to Janie's house in order to make it seem as if she is stopping over there by accident. This way, the others couldn't ask Pheoby for gossip.

5.   Janie doesn't feel the need to wear mourning clothes because she is no longer grieving for Joe.

6.   The possum loses sense as it gets older, and Pheoby is worried that this is what is happening to Janie.

7.   Tea Cake isn't a businessman like Joe was. Janie is afraid that everyone will compare him to Joe if he started to run the store.

8.   Janie married Logan because Nanny fixed them up. She then married Joe and lived with financial security, which is what Nanny always wished for her. Now she intends to choose her own husband and live for the things that she wants to live for.

9.   Pheoby says that the "chicken drink water, but he don't pee-pee." Pheoby is also able to keep everything inside her, meaning that she can keep a secret.

10.   Janie has a new blue satin dress with high heels and jewelry. Tea Cake picked everything out for her to wear.

Suggested Essay Topics

1.   How does the town's opinion of Joe Starks change once Janie and Tea Cake's relationship is made public? Compare examples in this chapter with those in previous chapters.

2. Janie says that if Tea Cake loves property, "he ain't no different from all de rest of us." Do you find this statement to be cynical or common sense? Would Janie have thought this way if she didn't marry Joe? Use examples from the novel to support your position.

Chapter 13

New Character:

Mrs. Samuels: *A landlady in Jacksonville.*

Summary

A few days after the end of Chapter 12, Janie receives a letter from Tea Cake that says that he is in Jacksonville. Janie leaves for Jacksonville, and she and Tea Cake are married that same morning. Tea Cake then takes her to a room that he has rented from a widow. Pheoby insists that Janie hide two hundred dollars in a special pocket of her dress, just to be safe. After a week passes, Janie wants to tell Tea Cake about the money but isn't sure how to do it.

One morning Tea Cake goes out, saying that he will buy her some fish. When Janie realizes that it is already noon and he is still gone, she decides to get up anyway. While she is dressing, she discovers her money is gone. She cannot believe that he has stolen her money, so she searches the room but cannot find it. Her mind starts to wander as she waits for him to return and she begins to think about Annie Tyler. Mrs. Tyler was a widow who at 52 left town with a younger man called Who Flung. Who Flung took her to an old room in a "shabby house" and promised to marry her. He left her the next day, taking all of her money. Mrs. Tyler returned to town and soon died after that. Janie isn't worried about the money since she still has some left but prays that Tea Cake is all right and that he truly loves her.

Tea Cake finally returns in the evening to find Janie upset. He understands why she is upset and tells her what had happened. As he was getting ready to go he spied the money out of the corner of his eye and picked it up out of curiosity. When he realized that it was two hundred dollars, he became excited and felt "like letting

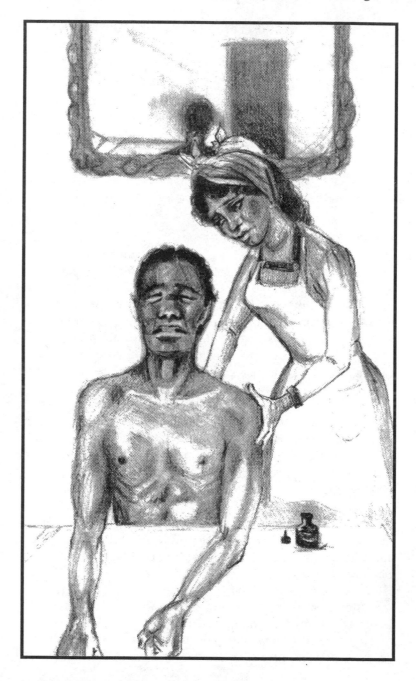

folks know who he was." After introducing himself to some local men, he decided to throw a huge party. While he was playing the guitar and singing, he decides to buy himself a guitar as well. After that wonderful day, "all he needed was a great big old hug and kiss from Janie."

Although Janie is relieved to see him again, she is upset that he had a party without inviting his own wife. Tea Cake apologizes, and tells her he was afraid that she wouldn't enjoy the sort of people with whom he usually socializes. Janie tells him that she wants "tuh partake wid everything." This relaxes Tea Cake, so he confides to her his plans to get back her money. He tells her that "you done married one uh de best gamblers God ever made."

When Tea Cake goes out to a planned game in order to win Janie's money back, Janie once again finds herself sitting in her room worried for Tea Cake. He finally returns after midnight with two razor-cuts in his back. As Janie is taking care of his wounds, he apologizes for being late. Even though he had won the money rather quickly, he gave the others a chance to win it back so that he couldn't be accused of cheating. He ended up with even more money, and finally got ready to leave when he was attacked from behind by one of the losers. Tea Cake took care of him quickly, and says that his own wounds aren't important, but Janie is crying from fear. Tea Cake comforts her and tells her to count the money. Tea Cake won three hundred and twenty-two dollars, and while they are counting, Janie confesses that she has a lot more money in the bank. Tea Cake returns Janie's two hundred dollars and tells her to put that money back in the bank because he intends to support her himself. Tea Cake tells her that they will go down to the Everglades in order to plant beans and "make money." Janie is now secure in her marriage and convinced that Tea Cake will not abandon her. As the chapter ends, Tea Cake drifts off to sleep, and "Janie looked down on him and felt a self-crushing love."

Analysis

Janie, after 20 years of living in Eatonville with Joe, finally leaves and pursues the same excitement and adventure she wanted when she came to Eatonville. In this chapter, Janie's doubts and fears are fully explored. When Tea Cake runs off and takes her money (or so she believes), her worst fears are justified. She is not worried so much about her money; she still has a lot in the bank. She is not worried about what the town will think, since she has no plans to return to Eatonville. What upsets her is that her trust and love will be lost if Tea Cake doesn't return.

The story of Annie Tyler plays over and over in her head. Pheoby Watson tried to warn Janie in the previous chapter by reminding her of Annie Tyler, who was swindled out of her money by a young man who pretended to be interested in her. Everybody knows what happened to her, because when the man left her, "she was broken and her pride was gone, so she told those who asked what had happened." What scares Janie the most is this loss of pride and independence, since losing Tea Cake after being so certain would be the cruelest thing that could happen to her. Annie Tyler "had waited all her life for something, and it killed her when it found her." Janie "done waited uh long time" as well, and she prays that the risk that she takes won't kill her as well.

When Tea Cake finally comes back, Janie is relieved and more certain about herself. She is, however, upset with him for having all that fun without giving her a chance to join in. After Joe put her on a pedestal and isolated her from any events and doings in Eatonville, the townspeople ironically believed she thought herself better than the town. Tea Cake didn't know if Janie would have liked such rowdiness, so Janie tells him in no uncertain terms that she wants to take part in everything he does. Once they reach this understanding, Tea Cake tells her that he gambles and will play in a game in order to win back her money.

Janie spends another night nervous for Tea Cake and deals with it with a long soliloquy, or extended monologue, in which she argues with "imaginary people who might try to criticize" Tea Cake for his lowly habits. The sort of people who would criticize Tea Cake are also the type of people who live in Eatonville, so Janie is defending herself against the people who disapprove of her. Janie wants these hypocrites to "learn to mind their own business," since jealousy is the root of all of their gossip. As she waits for her husband to return, she strengthens her position and justifies her choice by proving that her man is worth her trust.

Tea Cake finally returns, wounded but rich. As Janie counts their money and Tea Cake plans their future, Janie's soul "crawled out from its hiding place." After the ennui of running the store every day, Janie has felt a wide range of emotions. Through all of this, she had been cautious because of the doubt of the town. After Tea Cake proved himself, she feels free to bare her soul to him and to trust him in everything that they do.

Study Questions

1. Does anybody from Eatonville see Janie leave?
2. What does Janie send Pheoby after a week in Jacksonville?
3. Why does Mrs. Samuels ask Janie to drink coffee with her?
4. How did Annie Tyler get her money?
5. How much money does Janie still have in Eatonville?
6. How does Janie know Tea Cake is coming back?
7. What does Tea Cake do with the ugly women who want to get into the party?
8. What happens with two men who want to fight each other at Tea Cake's party?
9. What does God know about Tea Cake?
10. What is the name of the man who cuts Tea Cake with a razor?

Answers

1. Janie left early in the morning so there would be fewer people to see her go, "but the few who saw her leave bore plenty witness."
2. Janie sends Pheoby a greeting card.
3. Mrs. Samuels is a widow, and she considers it "bad" to drink your coffee alone in the morning.
4. Annie Tyler was a widow who got a lot of money from insurance.
5. Janie has twelve hundred dollars in the bank and ten dollars left in her pocket.
6. In the evening, Janie hears guitar playing out of her window. Janie jumps up when she hears Tea Cake singing and recognizes his voice.

7. Tea Cake pays each ugly women two dollars not to come into the party. One woman is so ugly that Tea Cake pays her five dollars.

8. Tea Cake forces them to kiss and make up. Neither man wants to do it, but everyone else thinks it is so funny that they force them to do it.

9. Janie says that "God knows Tea Cake wouldn't harm a fly."

10. Tea Cake calls the man who attacked him "Double-Ugly."

Suggested Essay Topics

1. Is Annie Tyler's story a cautionary tale? Do you think that we should feel sorry for her?

2. How does Janie react to Tea Cake's confessed "commonness"? Compare Tea Cake's description of himself with Joe Starks.

Chapter 14

New Characters:

Ed Dockery, Bootyny, and Sop-de-Bottom: *Three men who are playing a card game in the Everglades.*

Summary

Janie and Tea Cake get into the Everglades before the bean season starts, quickly find work with a planter, and move into one of the houses built alongside Lake Okechobee. Tea Cake plants beans while Janie settles into their new house. After the beans are planted, Tea Cake and Janie decide to pass the time by hunting. When Janie confesses that she doesn't know how to shoot, Tea Cake teaches her until she becomes a better shot than he is.

As they pass the time, more people come in from the surrounding areas and the area becomes more lively. The clubs are full of people every night, and Tea Cake and Janie become the "unauthorized center" of events. When it is time to pick the beans, Tea Cake finds that he is unable to control himself and can't get through a workday without missing Janie. He asks her to work on the farm with him, and she agrees.

This chapter also describes the general atmosphere of the town. One of the events in the town is a card game between three men which is filled with tension and excitement. As the cards fall, the men try to bluff and beat each other with words as well as cards. When the last card falls, everybody laughs and makes fun, showing that "no matter how rough it was, people seldom got mad, because everything was done for a laugh." Janie is loving every minute of her life here and thinks about what the residents of Eatonville would do if they could see her now. She decides that "she was sorry for her friends back there [in Eatonville] and scornful of the others."

Analysis

The setting of this novel dramatically changes with their arrival in the Everglades. The narrator speaks from Janie's perspective, and to Janie, everything is "big and new." This contrast in setting establishes a sense of adventure that was lacking in Eatonville; the reader senses the excitement of the unknown. When Janie and Tea Cake settle down to work, the beauty of the surroundings make this place seem almost idyllic, or idealized.

The society here in the Everglades has a slightly different set of values than Eatonville. Like Eatonville, the men are considered head of the household, and Tea Cake's popularity makes Janie popular as well. However, Janie's isolation makes her a target of resentment among the other workers. When Janie sat aloof in Eatonville because Joe isolated her, the other members of the community looked upon her with respect and awe. In the Everglades, Janie doesn't work on the farm because Tea Cake orders her to, but because they are living for themselves, they are unaware that her isolation is being interpreted as snobbery. Tea Cake asks Janie to work on the farm because he wants her to, not because the other residents demand it. Janie shows that she is more than willing to work on the farm, which quickly defuses the resentment and allows her to develop her own identity.

Tea Cake and Janie also show the reader that they are not willing to accept the traditional roles of a couple. Tea Cake tells Janie that he can't stand being without her, a sign of "weakness" according to the rules of marriage in this society, but a sign that Janie

appreciates. Tea Cake also teaches Janie to shoot, which is consistent with his character, since he has always thought of Janie as an equal. Janie, because of Tea Cake's acceptance, learns to not be afraid of speaking her mind and heartily begins to join in the stories and fun from which Joe had restricted her. The style of arguing here is also different; instead of the undercurrent of hatred that was always evident in Eatonville, the farmers here can "do the dozens" without hurting anyone's feelings. Since everyone here has roughly the same amount of money and everyone does the same sort of work, there is less jealousy here and friendships share a common bond. Tea Cake and Janie are loved because their nature makes them good companions.

In short, the Everglades is a utopia compared to Eatonville. A utopia is a perfect society, usually found in fictional works. Since a perfect society rarely lasts in a novel, the savvy reader would probably understand that everything is not as perfect as it seems, and would expect some conflicts to develop in the following chapters.

Study Questions

1. When does the bean season open?

2. Why is Tea Cake waiting for his new boss?

3. Why doesn't Tea Cake gamble while they are waiting for the beans to grow?

4. How does Tea Cake make Janie practice shooting?

5. What is Tea Cake's favorite dish?

6. Why does Janie make dessert every night?

7. What happens when the houses fill up?

8. Why do people come to Tea Cake and Janie's house every night?

9. How often does Tea Cake win at gambling?

10. Who won the card game?

Answers

1. The bean season opens near the end of September.

2. Tea Cake's boss left to get more seed.

3. Tea Cake hasn't been gambling because everyone at the farm is still poor.

4. He has Janie shoot at very small things in order to improve her aim.

5. Tea Cake's favorite dish is baked beans.

6. Tea Cake likes dessert because "it gives a man something to taper off on."

7. Once the houses fill up, the workers pay the boss so that they can sleep on his property in the open air.

8. Sometimes they come to hear and trade stories and jokes; sometimes they come to hear Tea Cake play the guitar, but usually they come to gamble.

9. Tea Cake won occasionally, but not too often, since there were a lot of good gamblers among the farmers.

10. Ed Dockery beat Sop-de-Bottom in the card game.

Suggested Essay Topics

1. Describe the hierarchy of this society. How are the most important people in this society determined?

2. Write a dialogue between two or more characters based upon the card game at the end of the chapter. Try to be consistent with the novel's use of dialogue.

Chapter 15

New Character:

Nunkie: *A young girl who is interested in Tea Cake.*

Summary

A problem arises on the farm when Nunkie, a girl who works in the fields, begins to play around with Tea Cake. Nunkie is clearly interested in him and even though Tea Cake fends her off, Janie starts to become suspicious. It becomes even worse when other people on the farm begin to notice the strange way Nunkie is acting.

One day Janie notices both Tea Cake and Nunkie are missing from the farm. She hurries to a field and sees Tea Cake struggling with Nunkie over some working tickets which she took from him. Janie chases Nunkie off and starts to fight Tea Cake in their quarters. Tea Cake holds Janie in his arms while she is flailing away, but eventually her hatred turns to passion. The next day, Janie asks Tea Cake if he loves Nunkie, and Tea Cake denies ever being interested in her.

Analysis

In this chapter, "Janie learned what it felt like to be jealous." Nunkie's behavior is clearly socially unacceptable, but the other townspeople don't seem to care enough to interfere, even though they do begin to talk about it. Janie takes it upon herself to fight both Nunkie and Tea Cake when she sees them together, showing that she is no longer willing to accept behavior that degrades her.

Even though the society was shown as somewhat idyllic in the previous chapter, the reader learns that not everyone is interested in seeing Tea Cake and Janie continue in their happy relationship. Jealousy and backbiting still exist here, as it would in any society. Janie and Tea Cake have encountered some resentment as a result of their wonderful life, and Nunkie provides the town with a wedge that they can use to drive in between the two.

Janie, however, is not willing to be passive in this situation. Her direct interference proves to Tea Cake and the others that Janie can

now exert some control over her situation. Tea Cake is innocent, but instead of proclaiming his innocence, he allows Janie to win. Tea Cake shows his love by not relying on a stereotypically male role; he could have deflected this criticism with self-righteousness. Instead, he lets Janie hit him until she gets tired, which shows that he is not afraid of her anger and willing to let her get angry. Their love is stronger than this petty jealousy and insistence on roles.

Study Questions

1. Describe Nunkie.
2. How would Nunkie play with Tea Cake?
3. How does Janie react to Nunkie's games?
4. How does Janie find out where Tea Cake is?
5. Why does Janie go home instead of to work?
6. What does Tea Cake do to keep Janie from running away?
7. How does Tea Cake "bruise" Janie's ears?
8. Does Janie believe that Tea Cake was ever interested in Nunkie?
9. Why does Janie want to hear Tea Cake's denial once again?
10. How does Tea Cake describe Nunkie to Janie?

Answers

1. She is a "little, chunky girl."
2. Nunkie would continue to hit Tea Cake and when he finally retaliated, she would fall down and cause him to help her get up. She would also tease him and provoke him to chase her.
3. Janie starts to be a little "snappish."
4. Janie asks Sop-de-Bottom, who points her to an adjacent field.
5. Janie leaves work because after seeing Tea Cake and Nunkie together "the sight of the fields and the other happy people was too much for her."

6. Tea Cake holds on to her wrists to keep her from escaping.

7. Tea Cake "bruises" Janie's ears by supposedly telling her the lie that he hasn't been seeing Nunkie.

8. Janie doesn't believe that Tea Cake was interested in Nunkie.

9. Janie wants Tea Cake to insult Nunkie for her, so that she can "crow" over Nunkie.

10. Tea Cake compares Nunkie to a chopping block.

Suggested Essay Topics

1. Discuss how you would have handled the situation with Nunkie if you were Tea Cake. Also discuss the situation as if you were Janie.

2. How do you think Janie feels in the town now? Does this situation demean Janie or Nunkie in the eyes of the farmers? Explain your answer.

Chapter 16

New Characters:

Mrs. and Mr. Turner: *A café owner and her husband.*

Summary

The season ends and most of the workers leave the Everglades. Janie and Tea Cake decide to stay because they want to work in the farm one more year. With less to do in the off-season, Janie spends more time in a café and begins to talk more with Mrs. Turner. Mrs. Turner is a light-skinned woman who wants to befriend Janie because she is also light-skinned. Mrs. Turner hates dark-skinned blacks and accuses them of "holding us back." Janie feels uncomfortable when she talks to her but doesn't know how to get rid of her.

Tea Cake hates Mrs. Turner, because she insults him at every opportunity. He also finds out that she is trying to introduce her brother to Janie in order to break up their marriage. Tea Cake runs

into Mr. Turner one time, intending to start a fight, but he sees that Mr. Turner is so henpecked and inoffensive that it wouldn't do any good. Tea Cake asks Janie to ignore her, and Janie readily agrees. However, Mrs. Turner simply ignores Janie's insults and bad manners because Janie is so light-skinned. As the summer ends and people return, Janie and Tea Cake do their best to ignore Mrs. Turner and enjoy their vacation.

Analysis

This chapter is mainly a forum for Mrs. Turner, who is a new antagonist in the novel. She has a bitter hatred for blacks, and dark-skinned blacks in particular. Her ironic name suggests that she is a traitor ("turner") against her own people, and her forced friendship with Janie makes Janie very uncomfortable, since Janie's alliance with Tea Cake directly goes against Mrs. Turner's philosophy. As a result, Mrs. Turner attempts to foil their marriage.

She, like the residents of Eatonville, is a symbol of power and the corruption that is usually connected with power. She uses her success to isolate herself from her race rather than share her wealth in order to make the collective rich. When she pulls herself up to a supposedly "higher level," she looks down at the others with scorn, just as Joe Starks felt himself to be superior. She sees Janie as a victim of the people of the Everglades; she believes that Tea Cake has "hypnotized" Janie. She feels "that she could remedy" the problem of her marriage with Tea Cake, indicating that she cannot believe that Janie is with him by her free choice. Mrs. Turner believes in her hierarchy "with fanatical earnestness," and directly associates whiteness with superiority. Therefore, Janie "should be cruel to her at times, just as she was cruel to those more negroid than herself in direct ratio to her negroness." This allows Mrs. Turner to stay Janie's friend even though Janie doesn't respect her. Mrs. Turner blames her character on her color, and since she can't change her own color, she becomes even more antagonistic to men like Tea Cake. Her self-hatred fuels her enmity to others.

Although Janie simply tries to ignore her, Tea Cake takes a more active role in defending himself. He wants to unite the workers with solid logic: "Since she hate black folks so, she don't need our money in her eatin' place."

Tea Cake wants to use the collective buying power of the community to match Mrs. Turner's power. His intelligent use of strength is a marked contrast to people like Joe Starks and Mrs. Turner, who had used wealth as a wedge to set themselves apart from society. Tea Cake wishes to exploit the positive aspects of their society, such as the friendship that exists among the workers.

Study Questions

1. Where do Tea Cake and Janie go now that the season is over and most of the people are leaving?

2. Describe Mrs. Turner.

3. How does Tea Cake joke about Mrs. Turner's appearance?

4. Mrs. Turner guesses to Janie that Tea Cake is very rich. Why?

5. What does Mrs. Turner believe should be done about the "black race"?

6. According to Janie, why do white people want to stay away from blacks?

7. Why is Mrs. Turner so proud of her brother?

8. What does Tea Cake intend to do about Mrs. Turner's insults?

9. Why does Tea Cake accuse Mrs. Turner of "making God look foolish"?

10. How does Mrs. Turner feel when she is with Janie?

Answers

1. Tea Cake and Janie spend a lot of time with the Bahaman workers, the so-called "Saws." They would put on a dance almost every evening.

2. Mrs. Turner is a woman with a "milky" color who always sticks out her pelvis as if "she [was] conscious of it."

3. Tea Cake thinks that Mrs. Turner must have been kicked in the backside by a cow to get that shape. He also calls her "an ironing board with things throwed at it."

4. It amazes Mrs. Turner that someone as light as Janie would

choose someone who looks like Tea Cake without an ulterior motive.

5. Mrs. Turner believes it is necessary for blacks to "lighten up de race" and that light-skinned blacks should "class off" from dark-skinned blacks.

6. Janie figures that whites hate blacks because most blacks are "too poor."

7. Mrs. Turner claims that her brother once won a debate against Booker T. Washington.

8. Tea Cake intends to boycott her café and tell his friends to stay away from the café as well.

9. Mrs. Turner is able to "find fault with everything" that God made.

10. Mrs. Turner feels that when she is with Janie she becomes "whiter," with straight hair and Caucasian features.

Suggested Essay Topics

1. Research the life of Booker T. Washington, and comment on Mrs. Turner's interpretation of his accomplishments.

2. How does Mrs. Turner's relationship with her husband affect her character? Discuss their roles in their marriage, and compare them to other couples in the chapter.

Chapter 17

New Characters:

Stew Beef: *A worker and friend of Tea Cake.*

Coodemay and Sterrett: *Two would-be patrons of Mrs. Turner's café.*

Summary

The new season starts, and Tea Cake and Janie are reunited with their old friends. Tea Cake is still harassed by Mrs. Turner and her desire to introduce Janie to her brother. When Mrs. Turner

brings her brother over to visit Janie, Tea Cake decides to slap Janie "to show he was boss." As a result, Mrs. Turner's brother leaves them alone, and the farmers talk enviously about Tea Cake and Janie and their marriage.

As Sop-de-Bottom talks with Tea Cake, they decide that Mrs. Turner and her family are nothing but trouble and devise a plan to force them out of the Everglades. The workers are all paid on Saturday, and they quickly move among the "jooks" in order to enjoy themselves. That evening in the café, Tea Cake and several of his friends are eating when two other friends, Coodemay and Sterrett, enter. Coodemay quickly starts a fight, and Tea Cake tries to interfere, saying that "Mis' Turner is too nice a woman" to have men fighting in her place. As Tea Cake tries to throw out Coodemay and Sterrett, an even larger fight quickly ensues and Mrs. Turner's café is destroyed in the process. After the fight is over, everyone makes up and leaves for another place. Mrs. Turner is left to yell at her husband.

Analysis

The chapter begins with a shock. After witnessing the understanding that existed between Tea Cake and Janie, readers are unhappy to learn that Tea Cake slaps Janie in this chapter, because we (rightfully) associate such behavior with spousal abuse. Tea Cake does it for a very subtle reason, a reason that the modern reader might not accept. They have lived their life openly, and Janie was free to visit whomever she had wanted. Tea Cake put absolutely no restraints on Janie because she wanted to take part in everything that her husband was doing. In return for this openness, Janie is taken advantage of by the Turners. They continue to harass her and Tea Cake with their constant attempts to break up their marriage. As we could also tell from the incident with Nunkie, the people in the Everglades also felt resentment because Tea Cake and Janie did not act like a conventional couple. The new people who try to make passes at Janie or Tea Cake are unaware of their love, although it "didn't take them long to be put right."

Tea Cake makes it clear that he didn't want to hit her, but felt it was necessary to "show dem Turners who is boss." Tea Cake was seen as a weak husband due to the freedom he allowed his wife to have, and perceived as vulnerable to efforts to break up their marriage. Tea Cake doesn't need to assert his authority; their relationship has always been based upon trust. However, in order to stop being harassed, Tea Cake decides to take an action that will be understood by society's code of marriage.

Ironically, Tea Cake's abuse strengthens his bond with Janie in the eyes of both men and women in their town. The women envy Janie because Tea Cake is seen as desirable, and his beating is still tame when compared to their husbands. The men envy Tea Cake because Janie doesn't resist when Tea Cake hits her. Once they act like a "normal" couple, "everybody talked about it the next day," as if they were always expected to be different. Sop-de-Bottom starts to trade war stories with Tea Cake about wife beating as if Tea Cake would understand now. The society starts to relax its restrictive mores because it is now clear that Tea Cake and Janie's relationship is a special case. All of this implies a mutual understanding between Tea Cake and Janie as well; the beating is never mentioned by Janie. They seem to understand that this is being done in order to placate the society in which they live.

The chapter's main focus is the town's revenge against the café. It was implied in the last chapter that Tea Cake was going to employ the collective power of the town against the Turners. The plot used to destroy the café is both humorous and ironic; the situation takes place on a weekend when most of the men are "drunk." This illustrates the hypocrisy of Mrs. Turner; even though she hated dark-skinned blacks because "dey laughs too much and dey laughs too loud," she was more than willing to endure the laughter as long as they gave her their money. In the fight, Tea Cake acts as the man who tries to interfere and save the café. This forces Mrs. Turner to look upon Tea Cake as her superior; when things get out of hand, she grabs Tea Cake in order to stop the fight. Not only is Mrs. Turner's social perspective changed due to the fight, but her position of power is also destroyed when her base for this power is destroyed. The town demonstrates their ability to work as a collective power.

Study Questions

1. How many times does Tea Cake slap Janie?

2. Why doesn't Sop-de-Bottom hit his wife anymore?

3. Why don't the police arrest drunks on the weekend?

4. Why is the whole gang at Mrs. Turner's café?

5. What do Sterrett and Coodemay order at the café?

6. What does Coodemay ask the waitress to do?

7. How does the fight start?

8. Why does Mrs. Turner try to refuse Tea Cake's help?

9. What happens when everyone decides to make up?

10. What do Coodemay and Sterrett do on Monday morning?

Answers

1. Tea Cake slaps her "two or three" times.

2. Sop-de-Bottom says that if he tried to hit his wife, not only would she yell so loud the whole county could hear her, she would also knock out his teeth.

3. There are too many drunk people for the jails to hold.

4. They say they are at the café in order to get away from the wives, but according to their plan, they going to pretend to fight in order to wreck the place.

5. Sterrett orders fried fish and coffee, while Coodemay orders beef stew and coffee.

6. Coodemay tells the waitress to hold the food for him while he eats, and the waitress refuses.

7. Coodemay tells Sop-de-Bottom to give him his chair, so that he can sit down. When Sop-de-Bottom refuses, Coodemay tries to push him out of the chair, and the others soon join in.

8. Mrs. Turner soon realizes that Tea Cake's attempted interference is just making the boys fight harder, and it is destroying her café more quickly.

9. Coodemay and Sterrett take everybody to old man Vickers in order to treat them to some drinks.

10. Coodemay and Sterrett come into Mrs. Turner's café to apologize for their behavior. They both leave her five dollars.

Suggested Essay Topics

1. Why do you think Mr. Turner doesn't interfere at all in the fight in the café?

2. How do you think this fight affected Mrs. Turner? What will her attitude be about dark-skinned blacks in the future?

Chapter 18

New Character:

Motor Boat: *A fellow worker and friend of Tea Cake.*

Summary

Janie notices that the Seminoles that live around the area are starting to leave the Everglades. When she asks one of them, she is told that a hurricane is coming and they are moving to higher ground. The workers dismiss the warning, even though they notice animals leaving as well. When the sky gets dark a few days later, some workers get frightened and move east. One of the Bahaman workers asks Tea Cake and Janie if they would like to go with him, but they decide to stay, like most of the workers.

A few friends gather at the Woods' house for a party. Tea Cake and Motor Boat are caught up in a dice game and hardly notice that everyone else has left and the rain and wind have picked up strength. Tea Cake looks outside and quickly tells Janie to pack up their valuables. The water has already come up to their knees and Tea Cake is afraid that the dam holding the lake will burst and the lake will overflow. Tea Cake, Janie, and Motor Boat link arms and fight the hurricane winds as best they can, at the same time warning the others that the lake is about to flood the town.

They manage to reach an abandoned two-story house in a fairly safe place and drift off to sleep. Janie wakes up, however, to discover that the flood waters are reaching the house. Tea Cake and Janie decide to leave but Motor Boat is too tired. After saying goodbye, they leave for the bridge, which might be high enough to be safe.

Tea Cake and Janie, after a long struggle, manage to reach the bridge at Six Mile Bridge. However, it is crowded with whites and there is no place for them to rest. They try to go on, and head on to a road on which both sides are deeply covered with water. Tea Cake is very tired and has to stop to rest. Janie sees a piece of roofing and tries to get it so that she may cover him. When she picks it up, the winds blow it like a sail and the force pulls Janie over the side into the water. Janie sees a swimming cow with a dog lying on top of it. Tea Cake tells Janie to swim to the cow and hold on to the tail. Janie manages to grab the cow's tail, but the dog starts to attack her. The dog just misses her when Tea Cake comes up and stabs the dog with his knife. The dog bites him, just missing his eye, but Tea Cake stabs him a second time and kills him.

The next day, they finally make it to Palm Beach, and manage to get a place to sleep. Both of them are weary and thankful to be alive. Janie thanks Tea Cake for saving her life, but he says that she doesn't have to say anything "cause Ah'm heah, and then Ah want yuh tuh know it's uh man heah."

Analysis

With the problem of the Turners solved, it seems that Tea Cake and Janie can continue to love each other and play on the farm without interference. However, their utopia will soon be interrupted by the hurricane. Hurston uses foreshadowing in order to make the reader nervous; when the Native Americans and animals start to leave, the reader expects the hurricane to come.

The hurricane starts during one of the most exciting parties on the farm. However, the party begins to break up when the others notice the strength of the storm. Tea Cake and Motor Boat finally stop when they hear thunder outside, and Janie tells them to be quiet because "Ol' Massa is doin' His work now." The noise of

the storm makes the noise that they made at the party seem quite small by comparison. The implication is that this natural phenomenon is the product of God, which is instantly more impressive than anything that could be made by man. This storm can be a metaphor for the power of nature, the type of nature that we first read about in Janie's gentle bee. It is as if they understand the power of God for the first time. When the winds knock out the power, the others wonder if "He meant to measure their puny might against His." "Their eyes were watching God" in recognition of God's power, and the farmers understand with whom true power lies. This power is symbolized by the lake. The strength of the rushing water can knock any one person aside easily, and this illustrates the power that God and nature possess over human beings.

Tea Cake and Janie show their love for one another in the honesty of one's final words. Janie had been waiting for something to happen all of her life, but is now satisfied with Tea Cake. She doesn't care about her own death because she has seen light in her life and "so many people never see de light at all. You don't keer if you die at dusk," when your life has already been fulfilled. Having confessed their happiness with one another, they turn to face the storm.

Tea Cake shows his bravery by killing a vicious dog in order to save Janie's life. Although Tea Cake is wounded and their house is destroyed, they seem to survive the storm. In the denouement of the chapter, Tea Cake and Janie struggle to find a place to sleep.

Study Questions

1. How much money are the workers making picking beans?
2. Who begins to sing and dance to Tea Cake's guitar?
3. How much money does Tea Cake win from Motor Boat?
4. Why does Tea Cake go out while Janie is packing up their things?
5. How deep is the water when they leave the house?
6. What does Tea Cake have to abandon because of the strength of the storm?

7. How long and wide is Lake Okechobee according to Tea Cake?

8. What does Motor Boat plan to do if the water gets into the house?

9. Why does the cow panic when Janie grabs on to her tail?

10. How could that dog "raised hell" with Tea Cake?

Answers

1. The workers are making between seven and eight dollars a day.

2. Muck-Boy begins to sing and dance.

3. Tea Cake doesn't win any money; the game they play is a "show-off" game.

4. Tea Cake tries to find a car to take them to Palm Beach.

5. The water is "almost to their buttocks" as they leave their place.

6. Tea Cake is forced to throw away his guitar.

7. Lake Okechobee is 40 miles wide and 60 miles long.

8. Motor Boat will try to swim if the water reaches the house's second story.

9. The cow believes that she has been caught by an alligator.

10. Tea Cake would have been mad if the dog had bit him one inch higher, because the dog would then have probably taken out his eye.

Suggested Essay Topics

1. Compare the characterization of the animals in this chapter with previous chapters. How does the strength of the hurricane affect animals, and what is the significance of these symbols?

2. The line "their eyes were watching God" is found in this chapter. Why do you think this was the name of the novel?

3. How does Motor Boat deal with the disaster differently than Tea Cake? Compare and contrast the characters' handling of the crisis.

Chapter 19

New Characters:

Mr. Prescott: *A district attorney in the Everglades.*

Dr. Simmons: *A doctor who works in the Everglades.*

Summary

Two days later, Tea Cake decides to go out to look for work, despite Janie's warnings that every fit male is now being pressed into service to bury the dead. Two white men see Tea Cake and force him to work with other men. In the evening, Tea Cake gets worried about Janie and escapes. He rushes home to find Janie scared and crying, and they decide to return to the Everglades.

They return home, and Tea Cake reunites with most of his old friends. He quickly finds work, since people are needed to clear up and repair the dam. Three weeks later, he becomes sick. He has no appetite and cannot swallow anything. This scares Janie and she gets the doctor right away. Dr. Simmons sees him and immediately takes Janie outside. He gives Janie some pills and tells her that the dog that bit Tea Cake during the storm was rabid and Tea Cake will probably die. Janie is distraught, and wonders if God has some sort of plan for her.

Janie is nervous and decides to see the doctor about the serum. She is told that the doctor will be there tomorrow, and as she returns, she finds out from Tea Cake that Mrs. Turner's brother has returned. The mere mention of that name has caused Tea Cake, in his sickness, to become jealous, and Janie soothes him. As she puts her hand under his head, however, she feels a pistol underneath his pillow.

The next day, Janie wants to go to the doctor, but Tea Cake tells her to stay in the house. When he goes into the outhouse, Janie checks his gun, and turns the cylinder so that the three empty

chambers would fire first, giving her a warning. She also loads the rifle and hides it by the stove. Tea Cake comes to her while she washes the dishes and accuses her of treating him badly. When Janie hears the first empty click of the pistol, she quickly grabs the rifle and yells at Tea Cake to drop the pistol. After the third click, she understands that he is insane from sickness and can't do anything to control himself. Janie fires the rifle at the same time Tea Cake fires a live bullet, and Tea Cake falls over dead on top of Janie.

That very day, Janie is tried for his murder, and the workers around the Everglades are outraged. A white jury is quickly called and testimony is heard from both sides. Sop-de-Bottom tries to speak on behalf of the workers but is silenced by the judge. Janie is found not guilty and complaints are heard from the workers, saying that "'long as she don't shoot no white man she kin kill jus' as many niggers as she please."

Janie arranges to have Tea Cake buried in Palm Beach. She buys a new guitar and lays it in his hands. She bears no ill will to Tea Cake's friends and invites them all to the funeral. His funeral is a grand affair, with a band and ten cars full of friends and mourners. Janie, however, is dressed in her overalls rather than black because she "was too busy feeling grief to dress like grief."

Analysis

Tea Cake goes out and for the first time we meet white men in the novel. We immediately notice that these men seem alien in comparison with the other characters, and they impose the same sort of evil power that we have associated with other antagonists. There have been prejudiced characters in this novel, such as Joe Starks and Mrs. Turner, but these were blacks prejudiced against blacks. Their discrimination was covert, not racist by sight, but implied through a feeling of superiority over others. We see overt discrimination for the first time in the novel.

This prejudice is presented in the manner that the dead are buried. Every white person will get a pine coffin, while blacks are thrown into a mass grave and covered in lime. As Tea Cake works, he notices that the guards (who are all white) "think God don't know nothin' 'bout the Jim Crow law." His invocation of God shows the pettiness of the law of men, which the guards are claiming to

follow, as opposed to spiritual law. Their society follows a rigid hierarchy based upon color, not unlike the hierarchy in Mrs. Turner's philosophy. Like Mrs. Turner, this hierarchy is distasteful, and Tea Cake escapes this setting in which he is a second-class citizen.

Tea Cake and Janie immediately return to surroundings in which they feel comfortable, but Janie learns that Tea Cake contracted rabies from the dog in the hurricane. Hurston had used a false climax in the previous chapter to give the impression that the worst had passed for them. As a result, this news has a tremendous impact upon the reader. Janie herself feels betrayed by God and wonders "was He noticing what was going on around here?" Because she is a spiritual woman, she becomes resigned to fate and hopes that "maybe it was some big tease and when He saw it had gone far enough He'd give her a sign." She wants to believe that it isn't happening but uses her strength to try to accept it and cure her husband.

As Tea Cake becomes sicker and rumors start going around that Janie is seeing Mrs. Turner's brother, we see that Tea Cake has become jealous, something which he has never shown before. With this sickness of the mind, he starts to believe the lies spread by his so-called friends, who are once again showing the characteristics of the town. The fact that Tea Cake himself starts to believe this gossip proves that he is very ill. He starts to become one of the townspeople; he is "infected" with the same way of thinking that has caused the town to become suspicious of Janie. She forgives Tea Cake for his horrible words because she knows if he were healthy, he would never say these harmful things. It is this jealousy that threatens to consume him and causes him to try to kill Janie. Janie kills him because she loves him so; she can't bear to see him act this way and turn into one of the people that has degraded her all her life. Tea Cake's words are similar to Joe Starks when he was on his deathbed. She shoots Tea Cake in order to defend herself. Symbolically, she destroys the hateful and evil characters that she has suffered with her entire life, and in doing so, must sacrifice the one man she truly loved.

In the subsequent trial, we see the farmers rise as one against Janie. This anger is all that is left now that Tea Cake is gone, showing that Tea Cake was in fact, the moral center of the town. He was able to focus the energy of the town towards a positive goal, with him gone, all that is left is the anger and resentment, that is once again pointed at the defenseless Janie. Janie, used to being the target of blind rage, is able to forgive them and unite with them once again by sharing the bond of Tea Cake. His memory makes the workers ashamed for their hatred of Janie. Tea Cake's funeral becomes a glorious affair, and, in his spirit, the workers come hoping that Janie may forgive them for their actions. Tea Cake and Janie have shown that it is possible for people to move beyond petty jealousies and establish true love and respect for one another.

Study Questions

1. Why does Tea Cake believe he can walk through the streets without being forced to work?

2. What do the white men call Tea Cake?

3. Whom has Tea Cake seen alive, and who has died in the flood?

4. What does Tea Cake refuse from Janie?

5. Whom does Janie meet as she goes to the see the doctor about the medicine?

6. Does the doctor have the medicine for Tea Cake?

7. Why does Tea Cake tell Janie not to work in the front yard?

8. What does Janie do after Tea Cake falls dead on her?

9. What is worse than death to Janie?

10. Why did Sop and the others try to hurt Janie?

Answers

1. Tea Cake thinks that the guards wouldn't bother him because he had money in his pocket and couldn't be mistaken for a tramp.

2. The white men call him Jim.

3. Tea Cake meets up with Stew Beef, Ed Dockery, Sop-de-Bottom, 'Lias, Coodemay, Bootyny, and Motor Boat when he returns to the Everglades. He also finds out that Sterrett died in the flood.

4. Tea Cake is so sick that he refuses a big pot of baked beans from Janie.

5. Janie meets Sop-de-Bottom and Dockery along the road as she goes to see the doctor.

6. There was no serum in Palm Beach, but the doctor has already wired Miami for the medicine.

7. Tea Cake wants to keep an eye on Janie.

8. Janie thanks him for giving her the chance to love somebody.

9. Janie is not afraid of death, but she is afraid of being found guilty of murder, because that would mean that no one believed that she loved Tea Cake.

10. The other workers tried to hurt her because they loved Tea Cake so much.

Suggested Essay Topics

1. How does the white society of the jury differ from the societies that we have already seen and commented upon? Compare and contrast the courtroom society with the Everglades society.

2. How is Janie's killing of Tea Cake an act of mercy? Use examples from the novel to support your conclusions.

Chapter 20

Summary

The other workers of the Everglades want to forget their cruelty to Janie, and they want Janie to forgive them. They blame Mrs. Turner's brother for starting the rumors and drive him from the Everglades. They also beg Janie to stay in the Everglades, but without Tea Cake, there is nothing left for Janie to see here. She gives away everything to Tea Cake's friends and returns home to Eatonville.

The setting abruptly changes to Janie, back in her house, talking to Pheoby. Janie's story is finished. Pheoby is inspired by Janie's

story and promises to defend her against anybody else in the town who might say something negative about her. Pheoby also says that after hearing Janie, "Ah ain't satisfied wid mahself no mo'". Janie tells Pheoby not to worry about the gossip hounds. Janie pays them no mind because they can't do anything except talk. Janie knows that "you got tuh go there tuh know there."

Pheoby leaves and Janie goes up to bed. Janie first relives Tea Cake's death and then feels his spirit in her bedroom. She realizes that Tea Cake "could never be dead until she herself had finished feeling and thinking." Content to have her memories, Janie calls "in her soul to come and see" the wonderful time she had with Tea Cake.

Analysis

In the denouement of the novel, Janie has evolved into a complete woman who is now able to control her life as she had wanted. The flashback is completed, and the reader now sees why Janie is content to live and why she is the moral superior to the people of Eatonville. Janie understands that most of the people won't learn anything from her story; the "sitters-and-talkers" will just look at her with envy. Pheoby, however, understands that the real lesson to be learned is that it is necessary to take the initiative for yourself. Janie is not affected by others anymore, and the moral code that the society lives by will never again intrude upon her desire to live as she wants.

With this control, her horizon is no longer a far away place. She wears her horizon "draped over her shoulder." This final image marks Janie's transition to a goddess; she now has the same kind of power over her internal world that God has over Earth. This self-fulfillment is rare to come by; it requires living by one's own moral code. The people in Eatonville couldn't live like this, and neither could the people in the Everglades (their mob-like attack on Mrs. Turner's brother proves this). Janie's life has now become the sort of life she had wanted to live ever since she saw the bee and flower while sitting underneath the pear tree. Learning how to live this way was the most difficult lesson she had to learn. Having learned this lesson, however, she can live the rest of her life happy.

Study Questions

1. How does Sop-de-Bottom explain the town's attack on Mrs. Turner's brother?

2. How does the town make itself feel better after what they did to Janie?

3. How long had the town's anger lasted against Janie?

4. What is the Everglades to Janie without Tea Cake?

5. What does Janie keep for herself from the Everglades?

6. What is love like, according to Janie?

7. What does Pheoby plan to do tomorrow?

8. What are the two things that everybody has to do for themselves?

9. What is Tea Cake wearing for a shawl?

10. Where is peace for Janie?

Answers

1. Sop-de-Bottom says that he wouldn't have believed the rumors if Mrs. Turner's brother hadn't asked about Janie the minute he arrived in the Everglades.

2. The men beat Mrs. Turner's brother and kick him out of town.

3. Their anger lasted two days.

4. The Everglades is now "a great expanse of black mud."

5. Janie keeps a packet of garden seed that Tea Cake bought but never had a chance to plant.

6. Janie says that love is like the sea. It is always moving and it continually changes.

7. Pheoby plans to make Sam take her fishing tomorrow.

8. Janie says that everyone has "tuh go tuh God, and they got tuh find out about livin' fuh theyselves."

9. Tea Cake is wearing the sun for a shawl.

10. Peace is in "the kiss of [Tea Cake's] memory."

Suggested Essay Topics

1.   Do you think that the ending of this novel is happy or tragic?

2.   What do you think will happen with Janie?

Sample Analytical Paper Topics

Topic #1

Throughout her life, Janie has to fight what is expected of her by other people. Follow her life in the novel, and comment on how she battles these perceptions.

Outline

I. Thesis Statement: *The people with whom Janie lived tried to restrict her to an understood, stereotypical role, but Janie was able to free herself from these accepted roles.*

II. Nanny

    A. Thinks a woman should be safe

    B. Encourages Janie to marry for convenience

    C. Is satisfied with Janie's life, though Janie herself is not

III. Logan

    A. Cannot understand why Janie won't act like his last wife

    B. Expects Janie to work without question

        1. Becomes more demanding when he feels threatened

        2. Treats Janie like property

    C. Janie leaves him for Joe Starks

IV. Joe Starks

    A. Entices Janie with talk of ambition and dreams

    B. Expects her to be content with his dreams

    C. Feels threatened by her refusal

        1. Tries to suppress her

        2. Becomes abusive when she retaliates

    D. His death liberates her

Topic #2

Compare the settings of the novel in terms of the system of power that is used in each society. How is power used in each society?

Outline

I. Thesis Statement: *The setting in the novel* Their Eyes Were Watching God *is directly related to the hierarchy of power that each location uses.*

II. Janie's pear tree

    A. The revelation is natural

    B. Nature is connected with beauty

    C. Contrast with Logan's farm

        1. Power is based upon usefulness

III. Eatonville

    A. Joe Starks is the central figure

        1. Achieves this power through accomplishment

        2. Earns the respect of the people

    B. Exploits his power for personal satisfaction

    C. His loss of power equals loss of life

IV. The Everglades

    A. No one is superior since everyone is poor

    B. Tea Cake and Janie become leaders due to personal charm

    C. People who have power become the enemy

        1. Mrs. Turner and her brother

        2. Janie, briefly, due to Tea Cake's death

V. The hurricane

    A. The ultimate force of nature

    B. The true killer of Tea Cake

    C. No one is able to utilize its force, since it cannot be exploited

    D. Makes everyone equal

Topic #3

Compare and contrast Tea Cake and Joe Starks, and specifically their relationships with Janie and others.

Outline

I. Thesis Statement: *Tea Cake and Joe Starks are two characters who, throughout the novel, have the opportunity to interact and form relationships with other characters. How they maintain their respective relationships provides insight to their character.*

II. Joe Starks

    A. Receives awe and respect

    B. Is envied because of his wealth

III. Tea Cake

    A. Is good-natured and "common"

    B. Makes friends easily

    C. Is respected because of his good nature

IV. How they maintain their relationships

    A. Joe Starks

        1. Bullies the town in order to get their respect

        2. Once he becomes old, he sacrifices his pride for phony respect

    B. Tea Cake

        1. Pays no mind to society or its social rules

        2. Uses genuine love to keep friends

V. Janie

    A. Joe Starks

        1. Prizes the respect of the town over his wife's love

        2. Janie is needed to stroke his ego

        3. Janie is placed away from the town as a "special possession" of Joe

    B. Tea Cake

        1. Janie is the most important person in his heart

        2. Doesn't need or want anyone else

SECTION FOUR

Bibliography

Quotations for *Their Eyes Were Watching God* were taken from the following edition:

Hurston, Zora Neale. *Their Eyes Were Watching God*. New York: Harper & Row, New York, 1937.

The following were consulted during the course of this work:

Gates, Jr., Henry Louis. "Zora Neale Hurston: 'A Negro Way of Saying,'" afterword from *Their Eyes Were Watching God*, 1990.

Hurston, Zora Neale. *Dust Tracks on a Road*. New York: Harper Perennial, New York, 1942.

REA's Test Preps
The Best in Test Preparation

- REA "Test Preps" are far **more** comprehensive than any other test preparation series
- Each book contains up to **eight** full-length practice exams based on the most recent exams
- **Every** type of question likely to be given on the exams is included
- Answers are accompanied by **full** and **detailed** explanations

REA has published over 60 Test Preparation volumes in several series. They include:

Advanced Placement Exams (APs)
Biology
Calculus AB & Calculus BC
Chemistry
Computer Science
English Language & Composition
English Literature & Composition
European History
Government & Politics
Physics
Psychology
Spanish Language
United States History

College Level Examination Program (CLEP)
American History I
Analysis & Interpretation of Literature
College Algebra
Freshman College Composition
General Examinations
Human Growth and Development
Introductory Sociology
Principles of Marketing

SAT II: Subject Tests
American History
Biology
Chemistry
French
German
Literature

SAT II: Subject Tests (continued)
Mathematics Level IC, IIC
Physics
Spanish
Writing

Graduate Record Exams (GREs)
Biology
Chemistry
Computer Science
Economics
Engineering
General
History
Literature in English
Mathematics
Physics
Political Science
Psychology
Sociology

ACT - American College Testing Assessment

ASVAB - Armed Service Vocational Aptitude Battery

CBEST - California Basic Educational Skills Test

CDL - Commercial Driver's License Exam

CLAST - College Level Academic Skills Test

ELM - Entry Level Mathematics

ExCET - Exam for Certification Educators in Texas

FE (EIT) - Fundamentals of Engineering Exam

FE Review - Fundamentals of Engineering Review

GED - High School Equivalency Diploma Exam (US & Canada editions)

GMAT - Graduate Management Admission Test

LSAT - Law School Admission

MAT - Miller Analogies Test

MCAT - Medical College Admission Test

MSAT - Multiple Subjects Assessment for Teachers

NTE - National Teachers Exam

PPST - Pre-Professional Skills Test

PSAT - Preliminary Scholastic Assessment Test

SAT I - Reasoning Test

SAT I - Quick Study & Review

TASP - Texas Academic Skills Program

TOEFL - Test of English as a Foreign Language

RESEARCH & EDUCATION ASSOCIATION
61 Ethel Road W. • Piscataway, New Jersey 08854
Phone: (908) 819-8880

Please send me more information about your Test Prep Books

Name _____

Address _____

City _____ State _____ Zip _____

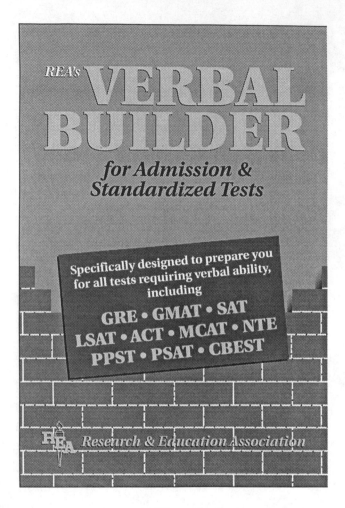

Available at your local bookstore or order directly from us by sending in coupon below.